MEDIEVAL HISTORY

By Ross J. S. Hoffman

Revised by James J. Flynn, Ph.D.

About the Author

1. <u>Present position</u>: Professor of Modern European History, Fordham University, Graduate School. Formerly taught at New York University.
2. <u>Publications:</u> Restoration (Sheed & Ward 1934); The Will to Freedom 1938); The Organic State (Sheed & Ward 1939); The Great Republic (Sheed & Ward 1942). Co-author: Burke's Politics (A. A. Knopf 1949). Has written articles and reviews for many of the historical quarterlies.

About the Reviser

1. <u>Present position:</u> Associate Professor of History and Government, Fordham University, School of Business. Formerly taught at Boston College, Northeastern University, and Babson Institute of Business Administration.
2. <u>Publications:</u> Articles published in historical periodicals. Member of the Editorial Board of "Social Studies."

About the Book

1. This outline has been arranged to meet the topic approach to be found in standard textbooks in Medieval History.
2. A list of the most useful books on special subjects are added for each chapter.
3. A tabulated table of references to the major textbooks aids the reader to more detailed explanations of the subject matter contained in each chapter of this outline.
4. Includes a complete section of questions with helpful hints on how to prepare for examinations.
5. A series of maps have been added to help bring to life the story of the Middle Ages.

LITTLEFIELD COLLEGE OUTLINES

A. W. LITTLEFIELD, *General Editor*

*Asterisk indicates titles in the new Students Outline Series

MEDIEVAL HISTORY

By Ross J. S. Hoffman, Ph.D.

FORDHAM UNIVERSITY

Revised by

James J. Flynn, Ph.D.

FORDHAM UNIVERSITY

1958

LITTLEFIELD, ADAMS & CO.

Ames, Iowa

ACKNOWLEDGMENTS

The map appearing opposite page 1 has been reproduced from *The World of the Middle Ages* by John L. Lamonte by permission of Appleton-Century-Crofts, Inc. Copyright, 1949 by Appleton-Century-Crofts, Inc.

The maps appearing on pages 48b, 75a, 85a, and 108b have been reproduced from *Medieval History* by Carl Stephenson by permission of Harper & Brothers. Copyright, 1951 by Harper & Brothers.

HOW TO USE THIS OUTLINE

The student seeks to master history by an understanding of man's past actions, and an ability to relate these actions to present-day experience. The understanding of history is made possible only when the material is properly arranged. The student using a work that has attempted to free him from unimportant historical data can give himself over completely to understanding history. However, the student may relate this knowledge to present-day experience only when he is well versed in both.

It is the purpose of this outline to aid the student in understanding and relating the material of Medieval History from the decline of the Roman Empire to the Italian Renaissance. To accomplish this task several features have been added.

1. All material has been eliminated except that considered essential by most teachers. In addition, the most important information has been emphasized by _underlining_ basic facts, names, and dates.

2. The material has been arranged in outline form, with headings and subheadings clearly indicated. The student following these headings develops for himself an easily memorized outline of the subject.

The benefits to be derived from these features demands that the student follow some definite plan in preparing for examinations. First, he should consider that the most important principle is that review should take place throughout the course. Periodic reviews strengthen understanding of the general make-up of the course. In this important function this outline will enable the student to restudy the material covered in his text and the material gathered in the collateral readings assigned.

Secondly, concise, pertinent notes made during the periodic reviews of the topics in this outline will facilitate the final review. This method will enable the student to recall the high spots of the course and supplement it with the more detailed subject matter of the course.

This outline gives additional aid to the student preparing for examinations by placing at the end of the book a supplementary reading list for each chapter. These additional reading helps should aid the student in choosing his essential outside readings. Lastly, this outline has prepared a number of possible examination questions on each chapter of the book. A careful study of these questions and an attempt to answer them to the best of the students' ability will aid in correcting defects before taking an actual examination.

As far as the actual taking of an examination, the techniques vary according to the kind of examination. However, in any examination there are two cardinal rules:

1. Carefully study all directions.
2. Plan to use all of the time allowed for writing the examination. Since most examinations represent the culmination of an activity that has taken considerable time and energy, failure to take advantage of the entire time allotted is a short sighted policy.

J. J. F.

CONTENTS

Standard Textbooks in
Medieval History

Listed below are the widely used textbooks that cover Medieval History from the Fourth to the Fifteenth Century. The table that follows indicates the exact pages in these texts that are summarized in this outline.

Hulme, Edward M., *The Middle Ages*, (New York: Henry Holt & Co., 1929).

La Monte, John L., *The World of the Middle Ages*, (New York: Appleton-Century-Crofts, Inc., 1949).

MacKinney, Loren C., *The Medieval World*, (New York: Farrar and Rinehart, 1938).

Munro, Dana C., and Sontag, Raymond J., *The Middle Ages*, (New York: D. Appleton-Century Co., 1928).

O'Sullivan, Jeremiah, and Burns, John F., *Medieval Europe*, (New York: F. S. Crofts & Co., 1943).

Sellery, George C., and Krey, A. C., *Medieval Foundations of Western Civilization*, (New York: Harper & Bros., 1929).

Stephenson, Carl, *Medieval History*, (New York: Harper & Bros., 1935).

Strayer, Joseph R., and Munro, Dana C., *The Middle Ages*, (New York: D. Appleton-Century Co., 1942).

Thompson, James W., *Economic and Social History of the Middle Ages*, (New York: The Century Company, 1928).

Thompson, James W., and Johnson, Edgar N., *An Introduction to Medieval Europe*, (New York: W. W. Norton, 1937).

Thorndike, Lynn, *Medieval Europe*, (New York: Houghton-Mifflin Co., 1928).

VALUABLE READING GUIDE TO IMPORTANT TEXTBOOKS

Find the Chapter in the outline and read down for textbook references to more extensive readings. Follow your textbook by correlating chapters indicated on the top line with those listed opposite the author's names in extreme left hand column. Other important books are listed in bibliography.

CHAPTER IN THIS OUTLINE	1	2	3	4	5	6	7	8	9	10	11	12
Hulme	27-44	45-77	110-129	135-148	150-164	166-187	214-237	239-256		276-295	297-323	325-410
Lamonte	3-19	20-30	36-40	42-52	51-70	29-32 32-35	94-104	152-166	167-169	170-179	206-224	176-184
MacKinney	34-54	55-77	104-118	119-139	140-160	78-103	161-177	178-198	207-211	188-196	216-238	370-390
Munro & Sontag	3-14	15-26	36-47	48-50	51-59	60-67	92-100	69-79	118-121	150-160	126-137	161-174
O'Sullivan & Burns	48-49	190-194	77-97	98-130	130-139	244-300	571-580	138-154	387-388	389-427	453-502	431-453
Sellery & Krey	1-20	51-55	87-100	21-39	32-37	55-61	48-53	62-76	78-81	82-99	77-81 136-154	100-123
Stephenson	3-22	36-44	45-58	59-79	105-127	160-176	135-152	177-201	229-243	249-250 299-319	246-271	392-404
Strayer & Munro	1-16	16-21	22-28	28-38	66-70	58-65	71-77	47-57	103-108	146-154	109-120	158-199
Thompson	12-21	23-37	38-51	52-66	67-72	73-82	96-107	83-93	115-126	127-144	165-187	252-266
Thompson & Johnson	5-12	26-45	64-86	87-116	117-152	194-227	155-163	228-262	263-276	356-362	290-365	362-390
Thorndike	60-74	95-116	40-59	117-127	128-153	109-112 157-168	172-191	192-215	216-231	227-229 260-265	232-255	280-299

CHAPTER IN THIS OUTLINE	13	14	15	16	17	18	19	20	21	22	23
Hulme	456-499	596-629	737-774	778-798 802-837	501-536	412-428 630-648	644-648	641-652	656-661	649-656	618-623
Lamonte	334-361	370-375	391-416	553-612	417-443	454-464 471-483	660-668 675-678	634-653	690-699	725-732	733-754
MacKinney	494-531	345-369	408-429	254-333	397-407	448-493	580-605	555-579	606-629	488-493	704-720
Munro & Sontag	241-255	341-353	354-365	366-376	284-299	175-203	414-427	455-471	442-454	214-224	486-517
O'Sullivan & Burns	592-609	514-530	476-494	530-551	419-451	392-418	652-672	673-728	631-651	713-716	627-633
Sellery & Krey	108-176	230-235	175-189	240-277	155-174 190-200	201-215	294-300	301-316	317-326	374-387	365-373
Stephenson	320-342	343-368	406-414 509-511	415-494	405-407 529-538	369-391	605-628	657-673	575-602	542-544 648-649	708-720
Strayer & Munro	219-246	191-199	286-257 337-343	246-269	142-158	270-296	457-471	407-427	480-491	492-497	497-523
Thompson	176-187	195-208	282-302	336-350	303-334	209-221	222-230	352-375	336-350	376-388	404-406
Thompson & Johnson	515-559	579-606	643-686	687-738	397-431	489-514	481-489	954-993	906-953	94-120	994-1036
Thorndike	301-326	327-356	434-453	373-433	434-439 461-470	474-510	511-531	560-575	548-559	182-190	576-613

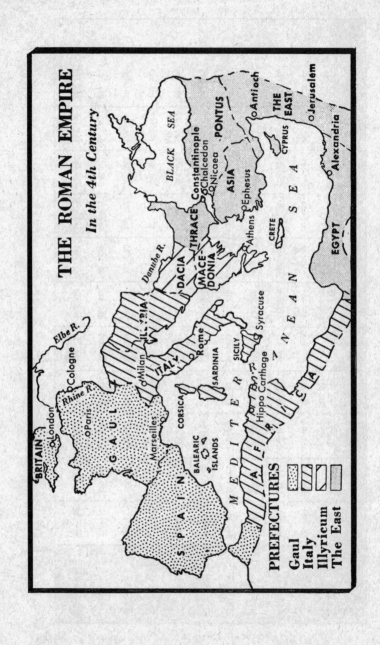

THE ROMAN EMPIRE

In the 4th Century

BRITAIN

London

Cologne

Rhine R.

Elbe R.

Paris

GAUL

Marseilles

SPAIN

BALEARIC
ISLANDS

CORSICA

SARDINIA

Milan

ILLYRIA

ITALY

Rome

DACIA

Danube R.

MACE-
DONIA

THRACE

BLACK SEA

Constantinople
Chalcedon
Nicaea

PONTUS

ASIA

Ephesus

Athens

CRETE

SICILY

Syracuse

Hippo Carthage

A
F
R
I
C
A

M E D I T E R R A N E A N   S E A

THE
EAST

CYPRUS

Antioch

Jerusalem

Alexandria

EGYPT

PREFECTURES

Gaul
Italy
Illyricum
The East

CHAPTER I

THE ROMAN EMPIRE IN DECLINE

I. <u>MEDIEVAL HISTORY BEGAN DURING LATER ROMAN EMPIRE, C. 300-600 A.D.</u>

  a. Roman political organization of the Mediterranean world crumbled.

  b. Ancient culture was profoundly modified by
    1. The victorious spread of Christianity.
    2. The arrival of numerous barbarian nations not previously under Roman dominion.

  c. Three chief formative elements in medieval history:
    1. The ancient civilization of the Roman Empire.
    2. The Christian Church.
    3. The new barbarian nations.

  d. Synthesis of medieval history constituted by interaction upon one another of the above elements.

II. <u>CIVILIZATION OF ROMAN EMPIRE WAS GRECO-ROMAN</u>

  a. It was an outgrowth and continuation (under Roman organization) of the Hellenistic civilization.
    1. Greek culture had disseminated and blended itself with the various ancient cultures of the eastern Mediterranean countries, *c.* 300-200 B.C.
      (a) Resulted in a ripened, cosmopolitan civilization, urbanized, with capitalistic economy and high level of material wealth, advanced in science, philosophy, and the arts.
      (b) City-state of Rome for long hardly more than a frontier outpost of Hellenistic life.
    2. Military, political, organizing genius of Rome gradually brought Hellenistic world into single political entity.
      (a) Romans adopted more and more completely the Hellenistic culture.
      (b) Greek language was only important feature of Hellenistic culture not adopted by Romans.
    3. Latin tongue of Romans disseminated over the west as Greek earlier had been spread throughout the east.

b. Roman Empire extended Hellenistic culture (Latin-
ized in the transmission) to western Europe under
protection of strong political power.
1. In the process ancient culture was greatly enriched by
   (a) Development of Roman law.
   (b) Roman engineering construction.
   (c) Roman military science.
   (d) Roman political institutions and the great imperial
       tradition.

III. EVOLUTION OF ROMAN IMPERIAL CONSTITUTION
a. Roman constitution gradually became a princely
   absolutism in the four centuries from Augustus
   Cæsar (27 B.C. to A.D. 14) to occupation of Empire
   by barbarians.
   1. Rome rose to command of Mediterranean world as aris-
      tocratic republic.
   2. Grave political crises led to dictatorship towards begin-
      ning of Christian times.
      (a) Augustus Cæsar took full magisterial power, but
          without doing violence to visible republican forms of
          state.
b. Constitution subjected to severe strain in third century by series of grave problems: economic depression,
   barbarian attacks, provincial and military rebellions.
   1. Dissolution forestalled by reforms of Emperor Diocle-
      tian (284-305).
      (a) Suppressed disorders and revised administrative
          system.
      (b) Empire was made in law and fact an absolute
          monarchy.
c. Structure of Empire after Diocletian's reforms.
   1. Empire divided into four centralized governments
      called prefectures; over each an imperial prefect who
      was virtually a co-emperor.
   2. Prefectures were subdivided into fourteen dioceses with
      a vicar at the head of each.
   3. A diocese comprehended several provinces.
   4. Provincial governors responsible to vicars, vicars to
      prefects, and prefects to the Emperor.
d. The colligual Emperorship.
   1. Diocletian nominated a colleague, Maximian, to share

the imperial office, assigning him control over the Empire west of the Adriatic.

(a) These two, calling themselves *Augusti*, then named two assistants with the title of *Cæsar*.

(b) Diocletian's plan was that after a certain time the Augusti should retire in favor of the Cæsars, who in turn should appoint assistants and presumptive successors and in due time retire to private life.

(1) Heavy tasks of absolute government could thus be divided, the while a law of succession to the Empire (hitherto a serious need) was supplied.

(2) Plan proved impractical, owing to reluctance of subsequent Augusti to resign.

2. The practice of nominating a colleague remained a familiar feature of the imperial office.

e. The Roman capital moved to the east.

1. <u>Diocletian</u> took personal command of the Prefecture of the Orient, comprising southern Greece, Thrace, Western Asia, Egypt, and Cyrenaica.

(a) He regarded Greco-Oriental lands as the heart of the Empire.

(b) His palace at Nicomedia, adorned with oriental pomp and the ceremonial etiquette of the east, was for the time the chief seat of government in the Empire.

2. <u>Constantine</u> I, a generation later, also regarded the center of gravity in the Empire as being in the east.

(a) Founded the historic city of Constantinople on site of old Greek city of Byzantium, 330. Constantinople thereafter the permanent chief seat of government in entire Roman world.

IV. IMPERIAL HISTORY IN FOURTH CENTURY

a. Long civil war in Empire, 306-323, followed retirement of Diocletian and Maximian.

1. Powerful figure of Constantine I (the Great), emancipator of Christianity and first Roman Emperor to receive Christian baptism, now emerged.
Sole master of Empire, 323-337; ranks with Diocletian as a restorer of order and peace in Roman world.

b. Constantine's three sons shared imperial rule after 337.

1. Empire was reunited under one of them, <u>Constantine II</u>, in 350.

2. Julian, 361-363, is chiefly remembered for his apostasy from Christianity which had been vigorously supported by the house of Constantine I. Died fighting the Persians.

c. Jovian, 363-364, made peace with the Persians and restored official patronage to Christianity.

d. Next came Valentinian I, a rough soldier raised to the imperial throne by the Asian legions at Nicea.

    1. Assigned government of the east to his brother Valens and established himself at Milan.

    2. Valentinian died 375, almost simultaneously with cataclysmic invasion of Europe by Huns.

    3. Valens slain by Visigoths in battle of Adrianople, 378.

e. General collapse of imperial system delayed during reign of Emperor Theodosius I, 379-395, the last to maintain undivided rule over whole Empire.

V. DECLINE OF THE ROMAN EMPIRE

a. Economic decay.

    1. First noticeable in agriculture; destruction of small, free-hold farmers by large-scale agricultural capitalism exploiting slave labor.

      (a) Empire faced serious abandoned farms problem by third century.

      (b) In later Empire slaves began to give place to *coloni*, semi-free agricultural laborers bound to soil but possessing some personal privileges and property rights.

        (1) This failed to check agrarian decline, for farming methods remained primitive and soil was becoming exhausted.

    2. Commerce and industry adversely affected by:

      (a) Shrinking of agricultural markets.

      (b) Unfavorable balance of trade with the east, depleting money supply (especially in western provinces), lowering prices and hampering trade.

    3. Political disorders and increasing brigandage hurt economic life.

    4. Excessive fiscality of the government discouraged trade by drawing away its profits.

b. Decay of the cities.

    1. Principal key to ancient civilization found in the institution of the city-state: politically independent

municipality, in which flourished vigorous local patriotism and public spirit.

   (a) Roman Empire was largely an achievement of the patriotic devotion of Roman citizens to their city-state.

   (b) Empire during years of greatest prosperity was essentially a league of city-states upon which Roman power had been imposed.

2. In later Empire cities everywhere deteriorating, and for many reasons:

   (a) Growth of skepticism about pagan gods (everywhere local deities), together with spread of oriental religions of universalist character, had destructive effect upon civic religion.

   (b) Increasing imperial interference in affairs of municipalities steadily destroyed their autonomy and initiative.

   (c) Economic decline and race suicide decimated city populations.

c. Race suicide: population of whole Empire seriously declining for reasons not adequately understood. Perhaps this simple lack of men constitutes chief explanation for termination of Roman Empire.

d. Barbarization of Roman life: steady infiltration of barbarian peoples, especially Germans, in process since first century, A.D.

1. This greatly increased by fourth century, due chiefly to:

   (a) Colonization of depopulated agricultural lands.

   (b) Their extensive availability for imperial military service.

2. Barbarian element grew more conspicuous in Roman life as assimilative powers of people in the Empire declined.

3. Barbarization clearly evidenced in deterioration of public taste and in intellectual and artistic memorials of later imperial period.

e. The heavy hand of the state.

1. State swelled its activities and expenses; more and more it subordinated private interests to its own; it became official doctrine that the individual existed primarily for the state.

2. Paralyzing official hand laid on many phases of eco-

nomic and social life; government compelled private persons to give their services to state without remuneration and often with responsibility for financial losses.

  (a) Empire legislated to keep men at their appointed work, on the soil, at a trade, in a public office, etc.

  (b) Having imposed duties on individuals, classes, corporations, etc., state enacted laws to forbid desertion and dissolution.

  (c) Trades and offices were made hereditary and a rigidity of social structure promoted that dried up individual initiative.

f. Political disorders.

1. Barbarian attacks on frontier.
2. Provincial revolts and military rebellions.

  (a) Influential factor here was the changed character of imperial armies.

    (1) Had become professional soldiery recruited largely from barbarian mercenaries.

    (2) Had become a danger as well as protection to state.

g. Growth of aristocratic independence.

1. The *latifundium*, or large agricultural estate owned by an aristocratic landlord and cultivated by slaves or coloni, was characteristic of later Empire.
   Economic self-sufficiency developed on the *latifundia*.
2. The great lord often secured certain exemptions from jurisdiction of provincial governors and thus assumed a measure of political authority.

  (a) Both individuals and communities often sought his protection to escape duties and taxes imposed by state.

  (b) Power of imperial government thus was encroached upon by landed aristocracy.

3. One of the roots of medieval feudalism lay in this tendency.

h. The victorious spread of Christianity.

1. This was the most significant historical development of the age.
2. Victory of other-worldly religious philosophy over secular outlook of prosperous earlier centuries created fundamental change in character of Roman society.
   Christianity did not repudiate classic culture as a whole, but broke with much of it and radically altered ideas that lay at springs of human action.

CHAPTER II

THE CHRISTIAN CHURCH IN THE ROMAN EMPIRE

I. <u>RELIGIOUS SITUATION IN ROMAN EMPIRE</u>
   a. Marked development of religious skepticism.
      1. Various pagan cults lost vitality.
      2. Lively religion languished, especially among cultivated classes.
   b. Many people turned to new religions which came out of East.
      1. Empire steadily penetrated by eastern influences and eastern religions were among most important of these.
         (a) Principal ones were the worship of Mithras, of Dea Syra, of Isis, and Neo-Platonism, Judaism, and Christianity.
         All had some consolation for men driven towards despair by meaninglessness, frustration, and misery of their lives.

II. <u>JUDAIC ORIGINS OF CHRISTIANITY</u>
   a. Judaism, whence sprang Christianity, was an intensely national religion with definite rites and ceremonies, a powerful priesthood and codified law.
      1. Jews had undergone much suffering for preservation of their faith; their history full of sorrows.
      2. They lost national independence through being incorporated in Roman Empire, shortly before Christian era.
   b. Teaching mission of <u>Jesus of Nazareth</u> outraged priestly caste and culminated in His crucifixion (*c.* A.D. 29). Official persecution continued against disciples of Christ.
   c. Followers of Christ gained additional converts in Jerusalem and adjacent communities, and soon launched missionary activities beyond Judea.
      1. <u>Paul of Tarsus</u>, educated Jew and Roman citizen, strongly influenced by Hellenistic culture, ardent, mystical, able, was foremost apostolic missionary (died A.D. 67).
      2. Christian gospel carried through Roman world and transformed from a Jewish minority into a religion of universal salvation.
   d. Although theology of Church was a gradual historic growth, all the essential ideas of Christianity were contained in teaching of Paul and other Apostles.

1. God, Father and Creator of all men, grieving over fallen condition of His children, had incarnated Himself and come among them to live that they might know the way to salvation.

    (a) Jesus Christ, only begotten Son of God and God Himself, through His sacrificial agony on the cross, had atoned for the sins of the human race and purchased its redemption.

    (b) Advent of Christ marked institution of a new humanity, saved through Christ, members of a Kingdom of Heaven with Christ as their sovereign Lord. He was to be accepted, obeyed, and loved, and the reward for His followers was eternal bliss with God.

2. Much of Judaism carried over into the new faith, since the Jewish religion was regarded by Christians as containing God's basic law and as truly foreshadowing the Divine Incarnation.

III. EARLY SPREAD OF CHRISTIANITY

a. Took place with remarkable rapidity.

1. Christian communities throughout most of Empire by 100.
2. Earliest converts chiefly from lower classes.
3. Large Christian penetration of middle and upper classes in second and third centuries.
4. Growth of Christianity more rapid in towns than rural communities, latter being strongholds for ancient cults.

b. Causes for spread of Christianity.

1. Doctrines of life beyond grave, equality of all men in sight of God, cleansing from sin through Christ's precious blood, had powerful appeal to distressed, downtrodden, disinherited, despairing.
2. Inflexible zeal of the faithful conspired with their moral rectitude, spiritual courage, and charitable care for the poor and distressed, to draw men toward fold of Christ.
3. The union and discipline bequeathed by Apostles and continued by their successors.
4. Certain favorable conditions for spread of faith in the Roman world:

    (a) Roman unity, which made proselyting on a large scale possible.

    (b) Philosophic skepticism cleared the way by weakening pagan cults.

    (c) Other Oriental religions containing ideas and practices akin to Christianity.

    (d) Searching of hearts encouraged by general decline of Roman life.

    (e) Persecutions by the Roman state served both to purge and to advertise the Church.

IV. CONFLICT WITH THE ROMAN GOVERNMENT

  a. Christianity a challenge to the secular absolutism of the Roman Empire.

    1. Conception of membership in Kingdom of Heaven with Christ as King contained implicit antagonism to Roman ideal that highest obligation of citizen was to Cæsar. Had Church been willing to accommodate itself (as did the multifarious other religions of the Empire) to imperial state cult, it would have had the protection of the laws; but it would make no such compromise, and so was warred upon as an *imperium in imperio*, or state within the state.

  b. Official persecutions began with that of Nero in A.D. 64 and continued at infrequent intervals.

    1. Hostility of non-Christian populace often greater than that of Roman magistracy.

    2. First large-scale, general, official onslaught against whole Christian body instituted by Emperor Decius (250); persecution of Church then continued to be prominent feature of Roman history down to adoption of Constantine's policy of toleration.

V. CONSTANTINE I AND THE CHURCH

  a. Last great persecution in progress when Diocletian and Maximian retired (305) in favor of Galerius and Constantius. Galerius issued first imperial edict granting freedom of worship to Christians (311).

  b. Vastly more significant was Edict of Milan which came in 313 from Constantine and Licinius.

    1. After death of Constantius in 306 his son, Constantine, stationed at head of army in Britain, became involved in struggle for imperial succession.

    2. Crossing into Italy he defeated Maxentius, who had usurped Cæsarship in west, the final engagement being a great victory in 312 at the Milvian Bridge near Rome. Miraculous revelation said to have come to Constantine

on eve of this battle, foreshadowing his taking up defence of Christianity.

3. Constantine now sole master of west, with Licinius holding the east; they reigned together until 323.

4. In his rise to power Constantine had shown benevolent attitude toward Christianity and now saw fit to develop still further the toleration policy.

He and Licinius issued <u>Edict of Milan</u> removing all disabilities from Christians and enfranchising Church as a legally protected institution (313).

VI. CHRISTIANITY BECOMES STATE RELIGION

a. Church grew rapidly in membership under Constantine I. Constantine actively favored Church and was received into it himself. His sons who followed him in imperial office were also ardent supporters of Christianity.

b. But care had to be taken not to offend pagan sentiment too deeply.

c. Not until reign of Gratian (375-383) and Theodosius I (379-395) was state support entirely withdrawn from pagan temples and Christianity made the official creed of the Empire. Then began official attack on paganism and heretics within Christian fold.

VII. MAJOR FORMATIVE INFLUENCES IN EARLY CHRISTIANITY

a. Judaic influences.

1. Earliest Christians nearly all Jews; even when cast out of synagogues they continued Jewish ways and claimed to belong to Judaism.

2. Christianized Jews still adhered to Jewish sacred Scriptures.

(a) These had been translated into Greek (the Septuagint) for benefit of Jews dispersed through cities of east.

In this form Jewish Scriptures passed into Christian Bible as Old Testament.

b. Greek influences.

1. Early escape of Christianity into Greek-speaking world of eastern Mediterranean.

2. Speculative, philosophical, ripened Greek intellect embellished and refined Christian worship and thought.

c. <u>Roman influences.</u>
   1. Late in becoming manifest.
   2. Chiefly in growth of church organization and law.

VIII. ECCLESIASTICAL GOVERNMENT

a. Idea of organic unity implicit in Christianity from apostolic times; but growth of hierarchic government a gradual evolution.
   1. Need for strong ecclesiastical government grew steadily.
      (a) Protection against persecution.
      (b) Administration of property.
      (c) Preservation of faith against heresies.

b. <u>Bishops the chief ecclesiastical officers.</u>
   1. Consecrated successors to Apostles.
   2. Gradual evolution of their governing powers; became heads of finance and administration and overseers of discipline and doctrine.
   3. Almost every *civitas* by 400 had its bishop, who was head of Church in that district.
   4. Episcopacy came to constitute the whole territorial government of Church.
      Subordinated to it was hierarchy of lesser clerical officials.

c. <u>The Metropolitan authority.</u>
   1. Bishops in certain great cities rose to pre-eminence as Metropolitans or Archbishops.
   2. Especially did archbishops of cities where Church was of apostolic origin attain high place, e.g., Rome, Alexandria, Antioch.
      In fourth century Metropolitan of Constantinople also became pre-eminent.

d. <u>The Councils.</u>
   1. Practice of Christians meeting in assemblies to settle important questions arose very early.
   2. Multiplied and grew more extensive in territorial scope after 313.
   3. First ecumenical council, or council of whole church, held at Nicea in 325.
      Ecumenical councils summoned very infrequently; others of fourth and fifth centuries were: Constantinople, 381; Ephesus, 431, and Chalcedon, 451.
      (1) Principal purposes to outlaw heresies, reaffirm doctrine, maintain unity.

e. <u>The Roman Primacy.</u>
 1. Ranking bishop of Church at close of fourth century was Bishop of Rome, although he had not yet developed the extensive authority which time was to bring.
 2. Reasons for Roman primacy.
    (a) <u>St. Peter</u>, leader and "Prince of the Apostles," by divine appointment, the rock upon which the Church was founded (St. Matthew, XVI, 13-20), was generally held to have transferred his seat of authority from Antioch to Rome about A.D. 42. Peter's authority, it was widely held, had been transmitted to his successors in the Roman see.
    (b) Immense prestige of Rome made it a natural capital for the Church in the Roman Empire.
 3. The primacy more conspicuous in the west than in the east.
    (a) West lacking in great cities like Antioch, Alexandria, Constantinople—natural capitals of great geographic regions whose bishops would have prestige enough to vie with Rome.
    (b) Rome the only apostolic church in the west.

f. <u>The imperial power and the Church.</u>
 1. Long a part of Roman constitution that care of religion was a right of the state.
 2. Therefore natural that Emperors, although Christian, should regard themselves as having jurisdiction over Church.
    Emperors did exercise a very great measure of authority over Church in later Empire.
 3. But Church tended to insist on independence as a right, and stressed new doctrine of separation of temporal and spiritual powers.

IX. BEGINNINGS OF MONASTICISM

a. <u>Eastern origins of Christian monasticism.</u>
 1. First Christian monks appeared in Egypt.
    St. Anthony of Thebes initiated first great monastic movement, late third century.
 2. Leading organizer of eastern monasticism was St. Basil (329-379). His rule of wide influence.
 3. Extreme asceticism characteristic of much of eastern monasticism, in contrast with western monks; St. Simeon Stylites (395-451) the best example of this.

b. Monasticism carried to the west.
 1. St. Athanasius (297?-373) brought monks from Egypt to Rome in 341.
 2. Some forty years later St. Jerome (340-420) greatly stimulated enthusiasm for monastic life in west.
 3. By fifth century many wealthy Christians had begun converting palaces and villas into monasteries and had even taken to monastic life themselves.
  (a) Spread of monasticism no less rapid and universal than Christianity.
  (b) Every province knew monks by fifth century.
c. Eastern and western monasticism contrasted.
 1. West less harshly ascetic, more practical, less contemplative than east.
 2. West more effectively organized.
 3. In west monks became zealous partisans of Papacy; not so in east.

X. GREAT THEOLOGICAL CONTROVERSIES

 a. Early Christianity underwent many internal struggles occasioned by theological differences of opinion.
 b. Foremost conflicts over heresy in fourth and fifth centuries concerned Manicheism, Pelagianism, and Arianism.
 c. The Manicheans dated from third century, when their founder, Mani, taught in Persia.
  1. More a rival religion than a Christian heresy.
  2. Fundamental belief was in existence of two eternal principles, good and evil; material world, held to be evil, was creation of the god of the Old Testament which they rejected. But Manicheans cited New Testament as confirmation of their doctrine. They were strongly ascetic in their lives. St. Augustine for a time was one of them.
 d. Pelagianism took its name from Pelagius, a British monk of early fifth century. Essence of this was denial of original sin.
 e. Arianism very important in fourth century and later.
  1. Took name from Arius of Alexandria, its chief advocate.
  2. Principal doctrinal divergence from orthodoxy was contention that Christ, although the Son of God, was not con-substantial and co-eternal with Him.

3. Arianism condemned at Council of Nicea, 325; but continued to have important influence.
Arian missionaries active among German tribes, most of whom were first converted to Arian Christianity; hence significance of Arianism revived with barbarian invasions.

XI. THE CHURCH FATHERS

a. The leading writers and teachers of the early centuries whose works were regarded as sound and became courts of appeal in doctrinal disputes.
Many of them living at close of fourth century and were leading minds of the age, especially Jerome, Augustine, and Ambrose.

b. Many of Church fathers born of pagan parents and all were, if not converts, at least learned in pagan literature and philosophy.
They valued knowledge, not as end in itself, but as an aid to the faith; whatever in pagan civilization could be used toward that end was incorporated in their teaching, while all else was dismissed as dubious, dangerous, or heretical.

c. Most influential writer among Latin fathers was Saint Augustine, 354?-430.
   1. Of Christian parentage, but went from Manicheism to Neo-Platonism, to Christianity; then became Bishop of Hippo near Carthage and prolific writer.
   2. *The City of God* his most important work.
      (a) Visigoths sacked Rome in 410 and pagan cry went up that this was due to desertion of old gods. Augustine replied with great work of refutation; perhaps most influential writing in history of Latin Christendom.
      (b) Nothing better signalizes change in Roman world: a funeral oration on transient glories of Rome and pæan of joy in eternal glory of Christ's Church.

XII. THE HOLY SCRIPTURES

a. Christian Bible in established form by close of fourth century.

b. Consisted of Septuagint (Jewish scriptures) and New Testament.
   1. Latter a body of entirely Christian writings.

      (a) All of apostolic age.

      (b) Consists of four gospels, or accounts of life of Christ, apostolic letters, a historical sketch of acts of apostles and an apocalyptic document.

c. Early Christianity produced many writings not included in New Testament.

Determination of what should be included began to become definite by second century; Church selected and discarded what was deemed desirable and undesirable for an official collection of documents witnessing to the Christian revelation.

d. The Latin Vulgate.

    1. Official Latin Bible of medieval Church was work of St. Jerome.

      (a) On suggestion of Pope Damasus I, Jerome, late in fourth century, undertook to make new Latin translation of sacred scriptures.

      (b) Gradually this version supplanted all others; became known as the Vulgate.

CHAPTER III

THE BARBARIAN WORLD BEYOND THE EMPIRE

I. EMERGENCE OF THE GERMANS

a. Indo-European people whose earliest known homeland was in southern Scandinavia, Denmark, Baltic islands, and Baltic Germany east to the Oder River.

First known report of them there c. 300 B.C.

b. Restless and expanding people; in succeeding centuries pushed to the Rhineland, to the Danube, to Vistula and deep into central Europe.

First known appearance on borders of Mediterranean civilization c. 190 B.C. Came in conflict with Roman power less than century later.

II. SCANTY INFORMATION ABOUT EARLY GERMANS

a. Their history very obscure before they were brought within pale of Latin-Christian civilization. Left no written records of their earliest history.

   b. Principal sources of information:
     1. Archeological materials.
     2. Epic poetry written down in middle ages.
     3. Law codes (written down after invasion of Roman Empire).
     4. Scattered references to them in Roman and Greek records.
   c. Fullest descriptive accounts given by Julius Cæsar and Tacitus.
     Latter's *Germania* the only ancient work (*c.* 98 A.D.) written exclusively about the Germans.

III. EARLY CONFLICT OF GERMANS WITH ROME

   a. The German Cimbri, in alliance with the (probably Celtic) Teutons, defeated Roman army in Alps late second century B.C.; turned west, crossed Rhine, and collided with rising Roman power in Gaul. Attempted descent into Italy.
     Were destroyed by General Marius near Vercellæ in 101 B.C.
   b. Renewed conflict came with Cæsar's conquest of Gaul, 58-55 B.C.
     This made Rhine a Roman-German frontier.
   c. Augustus made similar frontier of upper Danube toward end first century B.C.
   d. Attempt made under Augustus to bring nearly all German tribes under Roman rule (16 B.C.-A.D. 9). But insurrection led by Arminius secured German liberty east of Rhine and north of Danube, A.D. 9.
   e. Rome organized whole left bank and part of right bank of Rhine into imperial provinces which survived to age of barbarian invasions.

IV. PRIMITIVE GERMANS AND THEIR CULTURE

   a. Physical appearance and mode of life.
     1. Blond, reddish hair and blue eyes, large bodies.
     2. Clothing of skins and (among more advanced tribes) woven cloth; primitive fondness for bright, ornamentive trinkets.
     3. Dwelt in small villages of rude, wooden, generally portable huts, or in caves and holes dug in ground.
     4. Domestic work, including that of fields, done by

women, children, aged and infirm, slaves; **the free able-bodied German primarily a warrior and hunter.**

b. No common level of culture.
  1. Germans in south and west had contacts with Celto-Roman world which had strong civilizing influence on them; those on Elbe and beyond much more primitive.
  2. When Germans first appeared in light of certain history they were in transition from pastoral, nomadic life to more settled life of agriculture.

c. Social institutions.
  1. Monogamic marriage customs.
    (a) Tacitus praised their sex morals.
    (b) Father the autocratic head of family.
  2. The clan or *Sippe*.
    (a) Association of kinsmen descended from common male ancestor.
    (b) Members had important mutual obligations:
      (1) Fought together in battle.
      (2) Stood together in lawsuits.
      (3) Clan the guardian of widows and orphans.
  3. Social Classes.
    (a) Free men, the backbone of tribe.
      (1) All men capable of bearing arms who had never known servitude.
      (2) Among free men was warrior aristocracy, called Ethelings.
    (b) Slaves.
      (1) War captives, purchased slaves, children of slaves, delinquent debtors, losing gamblers.
      (2) Had no position before law; masters had power of life and death over them.
    (c) Freedmen.
      (1) Ranked little above slaves; were excluded from tribal affairs.
      (2) Most trade in their hands.

V. POLITICAL INSTITUTIONS
  a. Organized into tribes, or nations.
    1. No unity among tribes save occasional alliances.
    2. Names of tribes gentile in origin; each tribe an organization of clans; membership in tribe gained only by birth and therefore could not be lost.

  b. Tribal constitutions.
    1. Popular basis for tribal government: the free men.
    2. Tribal state possessed little magisterial authority.

  3. Visible organization of tribe seen in popular assembly of free men.

  4. Kingship arose slowly and was elective.

   (a) No Germanic kings attained to absolutist powers in age before migrations.

   (b) Kingship evolved out of protracted warfare.

  5. The *comitatus,* an important aristocratic institution.

   (a) A private army, or war band, grouped around an outstanding chieftain as his sworn followers, or *thanes.*

   (b) Relation of personal loyalty and honor.

   (c) Many chieftains, through their thanes, founded tribal dynasties.

   (d) One of roots of medieval feudalism.

VI. EARLY GERMANIC LAW

 a. Customary.
 No written German codes until after nations settled in Roman Empire.

 b. Sacred.

  1. Bound up with religion, especially ancestor worship.

  2. Only priests could punish offenses against tribe.

 c. Personal rather than territorial.
 German viewed his law as birthright possession from which he could not separate himself; hence carried it with him wherever he went.

 d. Wide liberty for free men permitted.

 e. Most offenses, save treason, desertion, cowardice, and infamous crimes, regarded as crimes against individuals rather than against tribe.
 Hence punished by private vengeance, wherein lay reason for the widespread feuds. To curb feuds there developed the *wergeld*, or tariff of compensations for aggrieved parties.

 f. Germanic trials.

  1. Little appeal to evidence, but rather for divine judgments in behalf of plaintiff or defendant.

   (a) One or other required to take oath and support it by:

    (1) Compurgators, or oath-sharers.

    (2) Submission to ordeal.

   (b) Another method was the judicial duel.

VII. GERMANIC HEATHENISM
   a. Religion a polytheistic mixture of nature and ancestor worship.
   b. German land abounded in good and evil spirits of streams, forests, caves, etc.; trees, waters, groves, wells, etc., sacred to numerous deities.
      1. Dead thought to lead existence resembling mortal life; hovered about the living, making demands it was prudent to fulfill.
      2. Every hearthstone an altar to ancestral spirits.
      3. Each tribe had a god as remote ancestor.
   c. Certain great deities universally honored.
   d. Central feature of heathen worship was sacrifice accompanied by solemn chanting and dancing.
      1. What was offered on altar might be anything from gift of grain to a human being; slaughter of humans in religious sacrifice universal in barbaric age.
      2. A priesthood performed the sacrifices and consulted gods.
   e. Germanic heathenism weakening by age of migrations; most of nations that invaded Roman Empire at least partially converted to Christianity; but among Germans who did not migrate the old cults kept their vitality far into middle ages.

VIII. ROMAN CULTURAL INFLUENCES ON GERMAN PEOPLES
   a. Germans profoundly influenced by Celto-Roman world to south and west, *c.* 100 B.C.-A.D. 400.
   b. Germans learned use of coins as money, the art of writing, and many other elementary civilized practices.
   c. Left bank of Rhine, Moselle valley, upper Danube, were extensively Romanized.
      Here Germans first made acquaintance with urban life; many German cities of these regions are of Celto-Roman origin.
   d. Latin language spread along frontier, bearing new ideas and words to barbarian Germans.
   e. Border warfare endemic, frequently epidemic, and

from this Germans acquired something of Roman military arts.

f. Often sons of German chieftains taken as hostages and held within Empire for long periods; these learned Roman arts and, returning, exercised influence over fellow tribesmen.

Roman political agents, merchants, and missionaries worked similar influence.

g. Extensive trade between Germans and the Empire a great factor in disseminating Roman ideas in Germany.

h. Penetration of Christianity the most important of all Roman cultural influences to enter Germany.

    1. Little known of this, save famous mission of the Arian Gothic Bishop Ulfilas (311-381) who worked among the Gothic nation.

His translation of Holy Scriptures into Gothic vernacular is earliest example of writing in a Germanic language.

IX. PRESSURE OF GERMAN NATIONS ON ROMAN FRONTIER

a. German world penetrated by deep-seated restlessness.

    1. Pressure of population on subsistence: rudimentary agriculture, game exhaustion, cattle plague, multiplying numbers.

    2. Pressure of non-German peoples from east.

    3. Love of booty, adventure, warfare.

b. Swelling pressure of tribes on imperial frontier from latter second century A.D. onward.

    1. Marcomanni ravaged Danubian provinces and north Italy, 167-171.

    2. Allemani, in 213, invaded Rhætia and twenty years later the tithe lands between upper Rhine and Danube; settled there permanently in 258, thus wresting north base of Alps from Empire.

    3. Franks swept temporarily over Gaul, 253-259; same period saw heavy incursions of Goths south of lower Danube; imperial province of Dacia abandoned (c. 270) to Goths.

c. Roman frontier sagging badly when Huns burst into Europe and precipitated migration of German nations.

X. Other Historically Significant Barbarians

a. Barbarian people whom Greeks had called Scythians dwelt on northern and eastern coasts of Black Sea— the Russian plain, or Pontus Steppe.
   1. Long a threat to Greek civilization of Black Sea, Asia Minor, and Balkan peninsula.
   2. Known as <u>Sarmatians</u> in later Roman imperial times.
   3. Frequently collided with Germans of central Europe, especially when Goths in third century pushed toward Black Sea and lower Danube.

b. Fierce mounted Asiatic nomads dwelt in basin of Caspian and deserts of Turkestan.
   1. Primitive, cruel, warlike, filthy people; standing menace to civilized China, Persia, and India.
   2. Occasionally some great conqueror, called a *Khan*, would rise at head of vast horde and establish a temporary dominion.
   3. At intervals a great horde would sweep off afar on wild career of conquest.
      (a) This has resulted in many invasions of Europe.
      (b) Such an event was the cyclonic invasion of the Huns into the German-Roman world about A.D. 375.

Chapter IV

FOUNDING OF GERMANIC KINGDOMS IN THE ROMAN EMPIRE

I. Visigoth Migration. Establishment of Their Kingdom

a. West Goths, on eve of Hunnic invasion, dwelt north of Danube in former Roman province of Dacia.

b. Sought refuge against Huns south of Danube.
   1. Allowed to enter Moesia; soon began to ravage and plunder.
   2. Crossed Balkan mountains into Thrace and won battle of Adrianople (378) against armies of Valens.
   3. Huns, East Goths (Ostrogoths), and Alani (not Germans) occupied imperial lands north of Balkan mountains.

      4. Theodosius I (379-395) held Visigoths to some measure of peace and order until his death; but situation was always dangerous.

  c. <u>Alaric</u>, leader of Visigoths, failing to secure generalship in Roman army, and capitalizing rage of his nation over withdrawal of imperial tribute, led Goths on their historic migration through the Empire, 397ff.

      1. Ravaged most of Balkan peninsula.

      2. Then turned west toward Italy.

  d. <u>Visigothic sack of Rome in 410.</u>

      1. Resulted after several invasions of Italy.

      2. Honorius, Western Emperor, shut himself up in Ravenna.
March on Rome undertaken to force Honorius to grant tribute, land, and military employment to Alaric's people.

      3. Rome plundered for three days, after which Goths set out for wheatfields of Sicily and Africa.

      4. Ships destroyed and Alaric died before end of 410.

  e. Led by Ataulf, successor to Alaric, Goths roamed Italy a little longer; in 412 crossed into Gaul and then on into Spain.

      1. Conquered much of Spain from Vandals, Alani, and Suevi, who had recently overrun it.

      2. Established kingdom covering nearly all Spain and southwestern Gaul, with capital at Toulouse.

II. MIGRATION OF VANDALS AND FOUNDING OF KINGDOM

  a. <u>Vandals</u> stationed in Roman province of Pannonia on Danube, as allies of Rome and defenders of frontier, late fourth century; example of Alaric set them in motion.

  b. Moved west with Suevi and Alani; after long circuit through northern Gaul they entered Spain.

  c. Crossed to Mediterranean Africa under their greatest leader, Gaiseric, in 429.

      1. Swept across Mauretania and Numidia and laid siege to Hippo (which fell in 430). St. Augustine, Bishop of Hippo, died during siege.

      2. Captured Carthage (439), which became capital of the Vandal Kingdom, a formidable fifth century power.

d. Vandals became noted Mediterranean pirates.
1. Captured Mediterranean islands; terrorized western waters.
2. Sacked Rome in 455.

III. CAREER OF THE BURGUNDIANS
a. Their earliest known home, as also that of Vandals and Goths, was in marshes of lower Vistula River; but toward end of third century they had migrated toward the Rhine.
b. Got grant of land from Emperor Honorius in early fifth century and probably began settled life around Worms.
From there spread out to west, and into valleys of Saone and Rhone; this took place about time of establishment of Visigoths in southwestern Gaul. This country ever since called Burgundy.
c. Burgundian Kingdom flourished in fifth century, but was conquered by Franks in sixth.
d. Burgundians left deep impress upon German traditions.
Among them took place events which inspired great medieval German poems, notably the *Niebelungenlied*.

IV. HUNNIC EMPIRE AND ATTILA, THE SCOURGE OF EUROPE
a. Huns, on first entry into Europe, on friendly terms with Roman Empire, but these soon faded.
1. When Attila became leader (433) they had possession of most of Danube valley; capital near present site of Buda Pest.
2. Power felt so widely that fabulous stories spread abroad of size of their kingdom.
3. Held many German nations subject; Attila dreamed of great empire like that of Rome.
b. Attila (449) invaded the west with vast army of Huns and Germans.
1. Repulsed decisively by Romans and Visigoths in battle of Châlons-sur-Marne.
2. Invaded Italy in 452.
(a) Fugitives from Aquileia, besieged by Huns, at this time founded city of Venice.
(b) Huns overran all of what is now called Lombardy.

(c) <u>Pope Leo I</u> went north and begged for mercy; Attila retired into central Europe.

c. Attila died 454 and his empire quickly crumbled; Huns then vanished as historic nationality.

  1. Terror of Attila's name faded and he appears in later German legends as quite amiable character.
  2. Germanic peoples held under Hun rule resumed their freedom.

V. <u>Barbarian Invasions of Britain</u>

a. Roman legions abandoned defense of province of Britain in 410.

  Followed obscure period in which land was harried by Picts and Scots.

b. Jutes from across North Sea (modern Denmark) seized Isle of Thanet, at mouth of Thames, and whole coast of Kent, c. 449.

c. Establishment of South Saxons (from Saxon Germany across North Sea) in Sussex c. 477; followed presently invasions and settlements of West Saxons and East Saxons in Hampshire and Essex.

d. East coast of Britain north of Essex seized by Angles (also from over North Sea) at unascertained dates.

e. Jutes, Saxons, and Angles came to be known amongst themselves as English; while among remaining Celto-Roman Britons they were called Saxons.

f. Fate of Roman Britain a sorry one; invaders non-Christians and very primitive.

g. Sixth century Britain a confused medley of barbarian principalities; history obscure.

VI. <u>Imperial History in West</u>, 395-476

a. Theodosius I succeeded in west by son Honorius, a child ruler, whose inglorious reign lasted until 423.

  1. In dealing with Visigothic invasion he shut himself up in Ravenna and entrusted defense of Italy to an able barbarian general, Stilicho.
  2. An intrigue led Honorius to have Stilicho murdered (408).

  Thus was lost an able general much needed in these disastrous years.

b. <u>Valentinian III,</u> cousin of Honorius, held western Empire, 423-455.

   1. Dominant personality during most of reign was his mother, Galla Placidia.

   2. In these times principal political problem was how imperial power might hold in check the new barbarian monarchies settled in the west.

   3. Outstanding military figure of age was Aëtius, hero of battle of Châlons against Huns; last of great Roman commanders in west.

c. Valentinian III murdered in 455; same year Rome sacked by Vandals; imperial power now virtually confined to Italy.

d. Real power in Italy now held by barbarian military commanders, who set up and put down puppet Emperors, 455ff.
Constantinople twice sought to nominate an imperial successor in west, but without permanent success.

e. End of imperial office in west in 476.

   1. Orestes, barbarian with Roman wife, in 475 set up his young son, Romulus Augustulus, as Emperor.

   2. Next year Odoacar secured power, slew Orestes, and deposed Romulus.

   3. Odoacar sent delegation to Constantinople declaring no need for Emperor in west; Emperor Zeno made Odoacar *Patrician* (or viceroy) of Italy.
Imperial administrative system continued in Italy with Odoacar at its head.

   4. No Roman Emperor save at Constantinople, from 476 to 800.

VII. <u>Rise of the Merovingian Frankish Kingdom</u>

a. <u>Two branches of Frankish people in fifth century:</u> Salians along North Sea, and Ripuarians along the Rhine.

   1. Both had pushed forward within the Empire in late fourth century; but although Ripuarians were driven back, Salians were allowed to remain as allies of Empire in northeast Gaul (roughly Belgium).

b. <u>Clovis, young Salian prince of Merovingian family,</u> came to power in 481 and began remarkable career.

   1. Led Frankish conquest of Roman Gaul north of Bur-

gundian and Visigothic kingdoms (the Kingdom of Syagrius) in 486.

2. Clovis joined with Ripuarians to hurl back westward advance of Allemani in upper Rhineland, 496.
Allemani tributary to Franks thereafter.

3. Burgundy made tributary to Clovis in 500.

4. Most of Visigothic Kingdom in Gaul annexed by Clovis in 507-8.

5. When he died in 511 Clovis was master of Gaul and Rhenish Germany; also sole king over both Salian and Ripuarian Franks.

6. Left large and strong kingdom to four sons.

c. Frankish conversion to Christianity.

1. Clovis converted in 496 after battle with Allemani; Frankish nation followed.

2. Franks identified their cause with that of Catholics of Gaul against Arian Burgundians and Visigoths.
Clovis assumed rôle of champion and liberator of Catholic Church.

3. Foundations laid for historic alliance between Frankish state and Catholic Church, leading to restoration of Empire in west in 800.

d. Frankland under Clovis' sons.

1. Divided rule; much quarreling among sons, all of whom were kings.

2. Theodoric, eldest son, conquered Thuringia, east of Rhine, in 530.

3. Burgundy completely taken over by Merovingians, 534.

4. Bavaria became tributary, 555.

5. Whole kingdom reunited under Lothair I, 558-61.

e. Austrasia, Neustria, and Burgundy.

1. With frequent divisions of territory among Merovingians, new names grew up.

2. Austrasia—East Frankish kingdom; capital center at Metz; predominantly Germanic.

3. Neustria—West Frankish kingdom; capital centers at Soissons and Paris; largely Gallo-Roman.

4. Burgundy, which retained its identity under new dynasty.

f. Frankland distracted by quarrels among Merovingian rulers in late sixth century; Clovis' state disintegrated.

VIII. Ostrogothic Kingdom in Italy, 489-534.

a. East Goths, or Ostrogoths, in Pannonia after dissolution of Hunnic Empire.   Threat to Constantinople.

b. Theodoric became king in 476.
1. Strongly influenced by Roman culture.
2. Offered services of his people to Emperor to expel other barbarians from Italy and hold it for Empire; Emperor glad to have Goths move farther west.
3. Whole nation invaded Italy (489); Odoacar overthrown and slain (493); Ostrogothic kingdom founded in Italy.

c. Theodoric most enlightened of barbarian kings.
1. His reign (493-523) an era of order and renewed prosperity in Italy.
2. Strove for peaceful amalgamation of his people with Romans, without undue Gothic oppression.

d. Theodoric acknowledged allegiance to Constantinople; entered into alliance relations with other new German monarchies; enjoyed hegemony in new political system of the west.

e. End of Theodoric's reign saw rise of bitter religious feud between Arian Goths and Catholic Romans.

f. Kingdom disintegrated under Theodoric's successors.

IX. Imperial Reconquest under Justinian

a. Great revival of imperial military and political power under Emperor Justinian, 527-565.

b. Major cause for attack upon Germanic powers was religion: Justinian, champion of Catholic orthodoxy, strove to overturn the politically powerful Arianism of Goths and Vandals.

c. Reconquest of North Africa.
1. Belisarius overthrew Vandal Kingdom, regaining for imperialist rule most of former African provinces, 534.
2. Followed quickly the recovery of Corsica, Sardinia, and Balearic Isles.

d. Recovery of Italy.
1. Belisarius next moved against Ostrogoths in 535, while other imperialist armies attacked Ostrogothic power in Dalmatia; by 540 Italy regained.
2. Under King Totila Goths reopened struggle successfully down to 551.

  3. Second complete imperialist conquest carried through by Narses, 552-555.

e. Meanwhile considerable strip of southeastern Visigothic Spain also seized by Justinian's army (554).

f. Government of west entrusted to a new official, *Exarch of Ravenna*; Narses first to possess the dignity.

X. LOMBARD CONQUEST OF ITALY

  a. Italy exhausted and impoverished by wars of imperial reconquest; easy prey for next invaders.

  b. Lombards by this time had moved into Pannonia.

  c. Under King Alboin, Lombards in 568 began conquest of Italy; took whole Po valley; swift and decisive work.

  Nearly all Italy fell under Lombard control with exception of Ravenna and its environs, Rome, and southern ends of peninsula. Po Valley, ever since called Lombardy, the center of their power; rest held by subject dukes of Lombard race.

XI. ROMAN-GERMAN WORLD ABOUT A.D 600

  a. In nominal Roman Empire stood group of Germanic kingdoms.

  1. Not very much known of these states because of scanty contemporary writing.

  2. Size of German element in them uncertain.

      (a) In much of Gaul, Italy, and Spain Latin element held its own fairly well.

      (b) German invaders usually constituted military, aristocratic, landlord class, although some dropped lower in social-economic scale.

  3. Although all German invaders were either pagans or Arian Christians by 600 Catholicism everywhere was gaining ascendancy.

  4. German kings availed themselves of surviving Roman political and administrative machinery and continued much of it.

      (a) Assumed absolutistic powers such as Romans had been accustomed to in government.

      (b) Sometimes took Roman titles.

      (c) Germans really venerated the Empire and never purposed to destroy it; rather thought of themselves as living within it.

5. Great legal confusion obtained owing to Germans bearing with them their ancient codes, the while much of Roman law survived.

6. Considerable survival of Roman culture other than law and administration, e.g., old amusements and popular customs.

   (a) But the last of classic Latin literature had been written and classic art had ceased.

   (b) Principal refuge of ancient culture in the Church, especially the monasteries, and in Eastern Roman Empire.

b. Eastern or Greek part of Empire continued under ruler at Constantinople, who was universally regarded as political head of the world.

CHAPTER V

THE BYZANTINE EMPIRE TO 802

I. ROMAN EMPIRE IN THE EAST

  a. Survived loss of western provinces to barbarians for about a thousand years (to 1453).

  b. Called Byzantine from former name of Constantinople: Byzantium.

  c. Grew more and more different in character and history from the west.

    1. West was Latin and now partly Germanized; east grew more Greek and Oriental.

    2. Important religious discrepancies appeared between east and west.

    3. History of Eastern Empire largely that of one city, Constantinople; history of west becomes that of various Latin and Teutonic nations.

II. BYZANTINE HISTORY, 395-527

  a. Reign of Emperor Arcadius, 395-408, son of Theodosius I; succeeded by Theodosius II, 408-450.

    1. How to divert German barbarians from vicinity of Constantinople to western provinces was major problem of these reigns.

    2. Theodosius II remembered for famous codification of Roman civil law (Theodosian Code) in 438.

   b. Succession of cautious and able emperors who paved
      way for imperial revival under Justinian (450-527).
III. REIGN OF THE EMPEROR JUSTINIAN, 527-565
   a. Reconquest of Africa, Italy, coastal Spain, etc., 534-
      555.
   b. The Persian wars.
      1. Victories in west seriously compromised by reverses ad-
         ministered in east by Persians.
      2. Ended in agreement to pay Persia annual tribute.
   c. Justinian and non-German barbarians.
      1. Filled region from Danube to Sea of Marmora with
         fortresses for defense against:
         (a) Slavs, a primitive Indo-European people who began
             to occupy parts of Balkan peninsula in sixth century.
         (b) Bulgars, Asiatic nomads akin to Huns.
         (c) Avars, also Asiatic nomads who, following in wake
             of Huns, terrorized central Europe in latter sixth
             century.
   d. Justinian's religious policy.
      1. At time of his accession the Monophysite heresy (single
         nature of Christ) raged in east while Arianism was
         dominant throughout much of west.
         Justinian a champion of orthodoxy and warred upon
         both of above heresies.
      2. Drew close to Roman papacy, which he also greatly
         dominated.
   e. Codification of Roman Law, the Corpus Juris Civilis.
      1. Partially begun under Theodosius II.
      2. Commission of lawyers collected all imperial statutes,
         omitting all repetitions and contradictions, 528-534.
      3. The jurist Tribonian in 530 headed commission to
         digest writings of Roman jurists; so resulted the Digest,
         or Pandects, completed 553.
      4. From this reign also date the Institutes, or textbook for
         law students, and the Novels, or additional laws issued
         during remainder of reign.
   f. Reformation of government.
      Abolition of sale of offices and suppression of unneces-
      sary officials.
   g. Building and engineering.
      1. Justinian a great road, bridge, and fortress builder.

2. Rebuilt much of Constantinople (after fire in 532); also Antioch and other Syrian cities.
3. Great age of church building; most famous that of Santa Sophia in Constantinople.
Marks beginning of Byzantine architecture.

h. Character of Justinian.

1. Love of order and system; capacity for details and energy for limitless work; ambitious.
2. Very religious and strongly interested in theology.
3. Capable of utilizing high talent.
4. Disposed to make position of Emperor loftier than ever; outdid Diocletian in oriental pomp and ceremonialism.
5. His famous wife, Theodora, exercised great influence over him.
6. His character very much blackened by Procopius in his *Secret History.*

IV. BYZANTINE DECLINE AFTER 565

a. Emperors succeeding Justinian: Justin II (565-578), Tiberius (578-582), Maurice (582-602), Phokas (602-610).

1. Barbarian irruptions and internal decline featured these reigns.
2. Misgovernment of Phokas led to his overthrow and founding of Heracliad dynasty.

b. Reign of Heraclius, 610-641.

1. Empire in anarchy on his accession.
2. Persians overran Syria, captured Jerusalem, and took Egypt, 614-616.
3. Heraclius, 622-627, recovered all and dealt nearly mortal blow to Persian power.

c. History of Empire from 641 to extinction of Heracliad dynasty in 717 a melancholy one.

1. Onslaught of Mohammedan Arabs; much territory permanently lost to Empire.
2. Slavic turbulence in Balkan hinterland.
3. Permanent settlement of Bulgars south of Danube in 679.

d. Reign of Leo III, the Isaurian, 717-41; period of revival.

1. Repulsed Moslems and Bulgars.
2. Reorganized army, administration, taxation.

      3. Laid heavy hand on ecclesiastical abuses; precipitated iconoclastic controversy, which cost him obedience of Italy and sowed further discord between church in east and west.

  e. <u>Empire continued to show strong vitality</u> on through rest of eighth century, withstanding internal dissensions and assaults from Moslems and Bulgars.

      1. At end of century reigned <u>Empress Irene</u>, mother of Constantine VI, ambitious despot who, having deposed son, reigned alone in defiance of historical tradition.

      2. Irene's abandonment of Isaurian religious reforms (iconoclasticism), her opposition to army and great landlords, as well as her crimes and suggested marriage with Charlemagne (new Emperor in west), led to her overthrow.

      Palace revolution in 802 enthroned Emperor Nicephorus I; marks turning point in Byzantine history.

V. THE GREAT IMPORTANCE OF BYZANTINE EMPIRE

  a. Eastern bulwark of Christendom and ancient civilization against barbarians on Danube, Persians and Moslems.

  b. Byzantine Empire for long led world in artistic workmanship in all fields: architecture, painting, sculpture, mosaics, carvings, enamel, etc.

  c. Maintained a rich, urban, commercial civilization throughout medieval times.

  d. Byzantine Empire one of the great bridges between antiquity and modern times.

CHAPTER VI

GROWTH OF THE PAPACY AND WESTERN MONASTICISM

I. THE PAPACY FROM LEO I TO GREGORY I

  a. <u>History of Roman Bishopric</u> a story of progressive evolution from *primacy* to *supremacy* over the Church.

      1. Much of this growth in early times very obscure.

b. <u>Leo I, 440-461</u>, appears as considerably more than primate of Church.
   1. Triumphantly asserted doctrine of Petrine *supremacy*.
   2. When Council of Chalcedon, 451, refused to recognize more than a *primacy* for Rome he declared the canon null and void.
   3. Secured from Valentinian III imperial edict declaring all western bishops subject to Rome, 455.

c. <u>Steady growth of appeals (to Rome)</u> from lesser bishops and provincial synods.
   1. Rome the only apostolic church in west.
   2. Bishops of east disposed to protest against exercise of this appellate jurisdiction.
   3. The jurisdiction fortified by collection of canons and decretals made by Dionysius Exiguus (*c.* 510) which disseminated idea of papal right to *declare* the law of the universal church.

d. <u>Fortunes of sixth century Papacy.</u>
   1. Catholic struggle against Arianism of barbarian nations strengthened papal leadership.
   2. Absence of Emperor from Italy after 476 partially emancipated Roman bishop from secular domination.
   3. Ecclesiastical supremacy of Papacy virtually established in western Christendom by time of Gregory I, 590-604.

e. <u>Beginnings of Papal temporal power in Rome.</u>
   1. Lombard invasion had reduced imperial rule in Italy to scattered regions and destroyed its effectiveness.
   In this situation Bishop of Rome gradually fell heir to temporal rule over ancient imperial capital. Such a situation had come by time of Gregory I.

II. <u>PONTIFICATE OF GREGORY I</u>
   a. <u>The situation in Italy</u>: land roughly divided among three political authorities:
      1. Lombard Kingdom with its outlying duchies.
      2. Imperial, or Byzantine Italy.
      3. Papal Rome and environs.
   b. <u>Landed endowments of Papacy.</u>
      1. Had grown enormously since time of Constantine I.
      2. Pope largest landed proprietor in Italy.
      3. Papal territories centered about Rome, but also were spread over Italy, Sardinia, Sicily, Gaul, Africa.

c. <u>Earlier life of Gregory</u>.
   1. Born in Rome *c.* 540 of old, rich, senatorial family.
   2. Named prefect of Rome by Emperor Justin II when only thirty years old.
   3. Upon falling heir to large fortune founded six monasteries in Sicily and that of St. Andrew in Rome.
   4. Resigned all wealth and retired as simple monk in St. Andrew's.
   5. <u>Pope Benedict I, 574-78</u>, drew him out into papal administrative service and then sent him as legate to Constantinople, 578-85.
   6. On return to Rome became abbot of St. Andrew's and in 590 elevated to Papacy.

d. <u>Characteristics of Gregory as Pope</u>.
   1. Reformed and systematized ritual music of Church.
   2. Outstanding promoter of monasticism.
   3. Great practical administrator of church offices and domains.
   4. Promoted strenuous missionary activity.
   5. Unswervingly maintained claims of papal *supremacy* and independence of ecclesiastical from secular powers.

e. <u>Gregory I and the Lombards</u>.
   1. Byzantine Emperors too occupied to send adequate forces against them; Exarch of Ravenna unable to protect Rome.
   2. Relations with Lombards reveal Papacy a virtually independent political power in Italy.
      (a) To save Rome, Gregory, in 592, made peace on own authority with Duke of Spoleto.
      (b) Through Gregory's mediation, peace made between Lombards and Empire, 599.
   3. By end of Gregory's reign conversion of Arian Lombards to Catholicism was well under way.

III. <u>BENEDICTINE MONASTICISM</u>
   a. St. Benedict of Nursia, 480-543.
      1. Like Gregory I, of noble Roman family.
      2. Organizer of great monastic community at Monte Cassino.
   b. The Benedictine Rule.
      1. Based on three fundamental vows:
         (a) Poverty.
         (b) Chastity.
         (c) Obedience.

2. Provided a strictly regulated life, including not only devotions but also manual labor and study.

3. Rule enjoined less harsh asceticism than was often found in early monastic life.

4. Monastery under government of elected abbot clothed with virtually absolute powers.

c. Each monastery, under Benedictine Rule, was to be self-governing and independent, save for episcopal supervision.

d. Benedictine Rule became widely known in time of Gregory I when Lombard attacks drove Monte Cassino monks to Rome.

Gregory, who was first monk to become Pope, greatly admired rule and promoted its adoption generally.

IV. CONVERSION OF ANGLO-SAXON ENGLAND

a. Beginning of this was one of most important developments of Gregory I's pontificate.

b. England at close of sixth century a group of non-Christian barbarian kingdoms.

Leading king was Ethelbert of Kent, who had married a Christian Frankish princess, Bertha.

c. St. Augustine of Canterbury.

1. In 597 headed monastic mission to England sent out by Pope.

   (a) Mission secured protection of Ethelbert and Bertha.

   (b) Founded monastery of Christ Church in Canterbury (Cantawabyrig, or *dwelling place of men of Kent*), site of later Canterbury cathedral.

2. Ethelbert and subjects very soon accepted Christianity. From Kent followed the conversion of Anglia, Wessex, Essex, Sussex, Mercia, Northumberland.

3. Canterbury henceforth the religious capital of England and seat of archbishopric.

Augustine first archbishop.

d. Progressive church growth in England in seventh century.

Rivalry of papal with Irish missionaries.

e. English monastic culture.

1. English monasteries of seventh and eighth centuries exhibited higher culture than in most western lands.

2. Best representative of this was the Venerable Bede, who

wrote history of English church, Bible commentaries, grammatical treatises, and works in natural science.

f. Missionary zeal of new English church.
From there proceeded chief missionaries who in eighth century evangelized Germany.

g. Papacy held in deepest veneration by Church of England.
1. Papal mission had created Church.
2. England became notable center of propaganda in behalf of papal *supremacy*.

V. CHRISTIAN CHURCH IN IRELAND
a. Status of Ireland
1. No heritage of Roman culture and tradition.
2. Consisted of five kingdoms, vaguely defined, within which flourished clan warfare.
3. In Roman times Ireland was called Scotia, and early in fifth century these Scots raided Roman Britain.
  (a) Their influx into Caledonia so great that country came to be known as Scotland.

b. St. Patrick, Apostle to Ireland, 390?-461.
1. Young Briton, son of Christian Roman decurion, captured in raid of Scots and held prisoner in Scotia, or Ireland; escaped to Gaul and there educated.
2. Returned to Ireland on religious mission.
  (a) Christianity already slightly known there.
  (b) Real conversion of Ireland the work of Patrick.

c. Divergences of Irish from Roman Christianity.
1. Due probably to isolation and to St. Patrick's contact in Gaul with other than Latin church forms.
2. Most important differences had to do with:
  (a) Calculation of date of Easter.
  (b) Form of monastic tonsure.
  (c) Nature of episcopal office.
3. Differences not ironed out until 733.

d. Irish missions in Britain and Scotland.
1. Very active in sixth and seventh centuries.
2. St. Columba founded Iona monastery in 563, whence came missionaries who converted Picts.
3. Came in conflict with Roman missionary movement begun by Gregory and Augustine in England. This settled in favor of Rome, 664.

e. <u>Irish missions on Continent.</u>
   1. St. Columba, 543-615, led mission into Brittany, Gaul, and Burgundy, c. 590.
      Founded important monasteries, notably Luxeuil and Fontaines.
   2. Christianity among Franks then in very demoralized state.
      Irish influence for moral improvement.
   3. Irish monks eventually aroused bitter opposition.
      (a) Resistance to episcopal authority.
      (b) Divergence in religious usages.
      (c) Attacks on Merovingian courts.
   4. Columba fled from Burgundy and engaged in missionary activity among Germans of upper Rhine and to the east.
      Several important monasteries in this region, notably St. Gall, were of Irish origin.
   5. Columba's last field of labor was in Lombardy.
      Founded monastery of Bobbio, a famous repository of MSS. of antiquity.

f. <u>Significance of Irish Church.</u>
   1. Maintained high measure of classical learning.
   2. Stimulated missionary spirit in medieval church.
   3. First maintained principle of monastic independence from episcopal control, which was later widely adopted.
   4. Church penitential system originated with Irish.

VI. <u>ANGLO-SAXON MISSIONS IN GERMANY</u>
   a. Notable group of men from new Church in England evangelized Germany east of Rhine, simultaneously with Frankish political conquests.
   b. Wilfrid of York in Frisia (Holland) in 677.
   c. St. Willibrod in 691 led mission to Frisia.
      Founded See of Utrecht, seat of chief missionary activity among Germans for several generations.
   d. Leading figure in whole movement was St. Boniface, of Crediton (680-755).
      1. Went to Frisia to serve under Willibrod, 716.
      2. Visited Rome, 718; there commissioned to evangelize Germany.
         (a) Gave rest of life to work in Germany.
         (b) Founded bishoprics of Würzburg, Marburg, Er-

furt, Eichstätt, and numerous monasteries, notably
Fulda.

(c) Became archbishop of Mainz and primate of German church.

3. Boniface the leading churchman north of Alps
    (a) As papal legate he reformed Frankish church.
    (b) Author of important political services.
        (1) Reconciled quarrel between Charles Martel and Church.
        (2) Probably played decisive rôle in Frankish change of dynasty in 752.

4. Boniface divested himself of all powers and honors in 753, returning to Frisian missionary field.
    (a) Martyred in 754.

e. Leaders of Anglo-Saxon missions supported by large number of English monks.

1. Powerful English influence on Continental Christianity.
2. They worked in closest accord with Rome.
   Important factor in strengthening papal supremacy.

VII. ICONOCLASTICISM AND THE PAPAL REVOLT AGAINST CONSTANTINOPLE

a. Trouble arose between Italy and Byzantine Empire in early eighth century.

1. Emperor Leo III, sought to remove images from churches throughout Empire (727).
   (a) New challenge to liberty of church.
   (b) General resistance to iconoclastic decrees, and in Italy Pope Gregory II placed himself at head of it.
   (c) Lombards seized occasion to attack imperial sections of Italy.

b. Popes Gregory II (715-731) and Gregory III (731-741) were in serious dilemma.

1. They sought both to pacify Lombards, and to resist iconoclastic Emperor.
2. In this situation they turned to Franks for aid.

VIII. FRANKISH-PAPAL ALLIANCE

a. Lombards turned against Rome and Papacy.
   Threatened independence of Papacy and absorbed lands claimed by Pope.

b. Gregory III in 739 appealed to Charles Martel, Frankish duke and mayor of the palace.

Charles refused, being busy with the Moslem danger
and quarrel with Frankish clergy.

c. <u>Lombard danger lasted down to 756</u>.
   1. King Aistulf (749-756) sought to unify all Italy.
      (a) Captured Ravenna in 751 and extinguished the
          Exarchate.
      (b) Came to Rome to force Pope Stephen II to recog-
          nize him as King of united Italy, 752.
   2. Stephen II sent plea to Franks for escort to Frank-
      land.
      Arrived at royal villa near Metz, 754; persuaded King
      Pepin I to invade Italy.
   3. Two Frankish expeditions coerced Lombards into sub-
      mission, 755-756.
      Lombards thereafter tributary to Franks.

d. <u>The donation of Pepin</u>.
   1. Pepin conferred territory of Exarchate of Ravenna on
      Pope as a temporal possession.
      This with Rome and its environs now under rule of
      Pope as temporal prince.
   2. Pepin's donation often regarded as foundation of papal
      state.

e. <u>Great significance of Frankish intervention in Italy</u>.
   1. Signalized Franko-Papal accord which led to Frankish
      restoration of Empire in west in 800.
   2. In theory Popes continued under Eastern Empire, but
      that was now tainted with heresy.

Chapter VII

MOHAMMED AND ISLAM

I. <u>Arabia before Mohammed</u>
   a. Arabia never included in great empires of antiquity.
      A vast peninsula separated from western Asia by
      large desert; has never been thoroughly explored.
   b. Politically a disunited land of clans.
      Many of these were desert nomads.
   c. Arab religion a varied polytheism.
      1. Memory of a better religious condition.
      2. Mecca universally venerated as religious capital.

II. MOHAMMED THE PROPHET; ISLAM AND THE KORAN

a. <u>Abul-Kassim</u> (Mohammed's real name) born in Mecca *c.* 570.

1. Member of aristocratic clan, but a poor man.
2. When twenty-five married rich widow, Khadija, for whom he became a caravan driver.
3. Religious ecstasies when about forty.

b. <u>Mohammed's new religion</u> known as Islam, meaning *submission to God.*

1. God, or *Allah,* is one, creator and ruler of all things; Islam is absolutely unitarian; Mohammed not a deity himself, but only a prophet.
2. There had been many prophets, six of whom were authors of new dispensations: Adam, Noah, Abraham, Moses, Jesus, and Mohammed.
3. Personal immortality promised to all believers; rewards and punishments after death.
4. Principal obligations of the faithful:
   (a) Testify that there is but one God.
   (b) Pray five times daily.
   (c) Give alms.
   (d) Observe the month's fast (Ramadan).
   (e) Make at least one pilgrimage to Mecca.

c. <u>Important social aspects of Islam</u>.

1. Prohibition of: intoxicating liquors, usury, adultery, exposure of female children, oppression of poor.
2. Polygamy permitted, with divorce very easy for men.

d. <u>The Koran</u>.

1. Holy scriptures of Islam, containing words and revelations of Mohammed.
2. Collected after his death.
3. Became basic law for all Islamic life: civil government, religious practice and belief, marriage, divorce, etc.

III. HEGIRA AND MILITANT ISLAM

a. Mohammed's first converts were in his own circle of family and relatives.

b. Presently met hostility of commercial aristocracy at Mecca.

In 622 he fled (the Hegira, or *flight of the prophet*) to Yathrib, since called Medina (from Medinat al nabi, *city of the prophet*). There well received. From 622 dates Mohammedan calendar.

   c. Islam now began to assume its warlike character.
1. Nourished by Arab blood feuds.
2. Arabs had long been given to plundering desert caravans, and those to and from Mecca were very rich. The unbelieving Mecca merchants might justly be attacked, so Allah revealed to Mohammed.

   d. In 630 Mohammed forced submission of Mecca and entered it as a prophet and king of all Arabia.

   e. Before his death in 632 Mohammed declared Islam should be carried to all nations.
Sent emissaries to Egypt, Byzantine, and Persian Empires demanding submission to Allah.

IV. RISE OF THE ARABIC EMPIRE

   a. Moslems (or Mohammedans) quickly fell upon Persian and Byzantine Empires, both exhausted by long wars.
1. Byzantine power driven from Syria, 639.
2. All Persian Empire conquered, 641.

   b. Egypt overrun, 643.
1. From there persistent onslaughts made on Byzantine power.
   (a) Constantinople besieged, 672-677.
   (b) Carthage permanently captured, 698.
   (c) Series of attacks launched on Sicily and southern Italy.

   c. All northern Mediterranean Africa conquered by end of seventh century.

   d. Moslems invade western Europe.
1. Led by Tarik, Moslems crossed to Gibraltar in 711 and destroyed Visigothic Kingdom.
2. By 725 had penetrated Gaul as far as Autun.
Defeated at Tours by Franks in 732; but not driven south of Pyrenees until 769.

   e. Islamic Empire ruled by Caliph (*successor to the prophet*), spanning three continents, reaching from Indus to Atlantic, embracing half ancient Roman world, had arisen.

V. LACK OF POLITICAL COHERENCE IN ISLAMIC WORLD

   a. Arab tribal jealousy and love of liberty prevented formation of coherent state in Arabia.

1. This same showed itself in inability to establish durable political empire.
2. Islam, moreover, torn from within soon after death of Mohammed.
    (a) *Shiites*, partisans of limiting succession to Caliphate to Mohammed's family, and
    (b) *Sunnites*, partisans of elective succession.

b. Reign of Omayyed Dynasty, 661-750.

1. Muawiya, governor of Syria, revolted and usurped Caliphate. Reigned 661-680 (Sunnite).
   Removed capital from Medina to Damascus, and founded hereditary dynasty.
2. Shiites persisted in opposition in Egypt, in parts of Arabia, and in Persia.
3. Misrule and internal feuds brought dynasty to end in 750.

c. Abbasid Dynasty succeeded.

1. Claimed descent from Abbas, uncle of Mohammed.
2. Came to power by exterminating virtually whole Omayyed family.
3. Moved capital from Damascus to Bagdad.

d. Political disruption of Islam.

1. One surviving Omayyed prince, Abd-el-Rahman, fled to Spain and there set up (756) independent Caliphate of Cordova.
2. Egypt lost to Bagdad Caliphs in 972 through setting up of Cairo Caliphate by Fatimites.
3. Disruptive internal forces set a limit to expansive power of Islam; it had reached its high-water mark by end of eighth century.

VI. ISLAMIC CIVILIZATION AND ITS INFLUENCE ON MEDIEVAL CHRISTENDOM

a. Moslem Arabs (or Saracens, *children of the desert*) were not barbarians.

1. Possessed own ripened culture and came into close contacts with seats of ancient civilization in Eastern Mediterranean and Orient.
2. Rivalled Romans as adapters and disseminators of civilization.
3. Under Abbasids Bagdad became greatest metropolis and commercial mart in world.
4. Islam united in commercial relations India and Far East with Spain and northwest Africa.

b. Islamic world from eighth to eleventh century was far advanced over western Christendom in agriculture, science, philosophic speculation, ancient learning, medicine, urban life, industry, and commerce.

 1. Under Omayyed dynasty at Cordova Spain was the richest and most advanced country of the west.

 2. Through Spain much of ancient civilization worked its way into western Christendom.

c. Some important effects of Islam on Christianity.

 1. Whole southern half of old Christian, Roman world subjected to rule of Caliph.

 Christianity not wiped out, but reduced to inferior position; its proselyting was halted and many activities curbed; many Christians apostatized; hence severe Christian set-back.

 2. Certain heretical sects benefited by coming under Moslem protection.

 3. Byzantine Empire and eastern church, both on ill terms with Rome, were crippled and dwarfed.

 Papacy left freer to establish its supremacy and take leadership of western Europe.

CHAPTER VIII

THE FRANKISH REVIVAL OF THE EMPIRE IN THE WEST

I. FRANKISH AFFAIRS UNDER LATER MEROVINGIAN KINGS

a. History of Franks, a sorry record of civil wars, 561-687

 1. Rivalry among members of royal family.

 2. Struggles of lay and clerical nobles against crown.

b. Emergence of Mayors of Palace.

 1. These officials at first mere chiefs of palace domestics.

 2. Became first ministers of crown.

 (a) Supervised administration of crown lands, and dispensed patronage of offices and lands.

c. Rise of Austrasian Mayors of Palace: the house of Charlemagne.

    1. Pepin of Landen, leader of Austrasian nobles, assumed office Mayor of Palace, 614.

    (a) Virtually ruled Austrasia to 639.

    (b) His son, Grimwald, succeeding him, in 658 tried to place his own son on throne.

    2. Pepin of Heristal, grandson of Pepin of Landen and Arnulf (Bishop of Metz in early seventh century), in 687 led Austrasian nobility to victory over Neustria at Testry.

    Pepin ruled all Frankland after this, as Austrasian Mayor of Palace. Inaugurated political revival which culminated with Charles the Great.

d. All Merovingian princes after Dagobert (died 639) were insignificant personalities.

II. FRANKISH HISTORY UNDER CHARLES MARTEL AND PEPIN I, 714-768

a. Charles Martel, son and successor of Pepin of Heristal as Mayor of Palace, 714-741.

    1. One of most vigorous of all Frankish leaders.

    2. Struck energetically at rebellious vassal peoples.

    3. Campaigned against Saxons.

    4. Faced great Saracen menace.

    (a) Defeated Moslems at Tours, 732.

    (b) At this time cavalry warfare adopted by Franks.

    (c) To meet Saracens Charles needed all possible resources, and for this he seized many church lands to distribute as military tenures to his lieutenants.

b. Pepin the Short, Mayor of Palace, 741-752.

    1. Charles Martel left authority divided between sons, Pepin and Carloman.

    (a) Latter retired to monastic life in 746.

    (b) Pepin left in sole command.

    2. Church was conciliated.

    (a) St. Boniface a dominant personality in these years.

    (b) Frankish Church drawn closer to Rome; Benedictine rule imposed on monasteries.

c. Pepin became King in 752.

    1. Merovingian authority now had long been a fiction.

    2. Church and Papacy favored new dynasty; revolution undertaken with papal approval.

    3. Dynasty came to be called Carolingian, from Charles the Great, its most illustrious member; although it was really the Arnulfing house.

d. Reign of King Pepin, 752-768.
   1. Intervention in Italy.
   2. Vigorous assertion of Frankish overlordship through-out Gaul and Germany.
   3. Last years saw bitter revolt in Aquitaine, and rupture of Bavarian allegiance.

III. FRANKISH INSTITUTIONS
   a. By eighth century they were much modified by con-tact with surviving Roman civilization.
      1. Romans had given allegiance to Frankish kings; all Church and government places open to them.
      2. Frankish state illustrates very well the fusion between Roman and German institutions.

   b. The Monarchy.
      1. Mixture of ancient German, Roman, and Biblical tra-ditions.
         Kingship hereditary, with election persisting as a form.
      2. Frankish kings sought to imitate Roman Emperors.
         (a) By striving for absolutism, issuing statutory de-crees (capitularies) like Emperors, and striving to continue Roman system of taxation.
         (b) Court life a crude imitation of imperial grandeur.
      3. Kings governed through:
         (a) Their counts, royal officials clothed with executive, military, judicial authority; had something of char-acter of Roman magistrates.
         (b) Tribal dukes; e.g., Thuringians, Alemanni, Bava-rians retained tribal autonomy and ducal dynasties under Frankish suzerainty.
      4. Crown maintained its system with revenues from royal domains, profits of justice, gifts and local services; di-rect taxation dwindled away.

   c. Law.
      1. Franks lived under own law, customary in origin and written down early in sixth century.
      2. Other peoples, including Romans, lived under their own laws, limited only by royal statutory ordinances.

   d. The Church.
      1. A major instrument of government; most effective agency for social control.
      2. The Church willingly allied itself with rulers who showed benevolence toward it.

IV. **ADDITIONAL FRANKISH CONQUESTS UNDER CHARLES THE GREAT, 768-814**

a. Pepin, dying in 768, left:

1. Austrasia and part of Aquitaine to one son, Charles.
2. Neustria and rest of Aquitaine to another son, Carloman.
3. Latter died in 771; all came to Charles.

b. Suppression of Aquitaine revolt.

Resulted in more effective rule of southwest Gaul and inclusion of Gascony in Frankish state.

c. The attack on Lombardy.

1. New appeals from Pope for aid against Lombards brought Charles into Italy in 774.
   (a) Siege of Pavia and defeat of Lombards, 776.
   (b) Charles himself assumed crown of Lombardy.
2. Charles renewed, or confirmed, Pepin's donation to Papacy.

d. The conquest of Saxony, 772-803.

1. Land of fierce Saxons was the lower valleys of Ems, Weser, and Elbe rivers.
   (a) People were very primitive, living very much as Germans had lived in time of Tacitus; still devoted to warlike pagan gods, to whom they offered up human sacrifices; fierce, defiant, untameable.
   (b) Menace to Frankland since sixth century.
2. Charles began to execute design of subjugating the whole nation, 772.
   (a) Long and bitter series of wars.
   (b) Saxons evolved unified leadership under Duke Widukind.
   (c) Saxon resistance broken only by methods of great brutality.
3. Christianity virtually imposed on Saxons by sword.
   (a) Powerful new bishoprics created: Minden, Paderborn, Halberstadt, Bremen, Verden, Osnabrück.
   (b) All Germany now included within Latin-Christian civilization.

e. The conquest of Bavaria.

1. Status of Bavaria: semi-independent duchy.
   (a) Under Duke Tassilo, during reign of Pepin, Bavaria showed disposition to cut loose from Frankish allegiance.
   (b) Charles forced Tassilo to renew his vassalage, 781.

2. Tassilo later broke loose again; Charles poured troops into Bavaria, 787, and forced his submission.

Tassilo deposed, 788; Bavaria placed under Frankish counts.

f. The Spanish March.

1. Charles was visited by Arab chieftains from Spain in 777; Abbasid partisans, sought his intervention against Ommeyad Caliphs at Cordova.

Seeing opportunity to liberate Christian population in Spain, Charles crossed Pyrenees in 778.

2. Little was accomplished; on the retreat rear-guard under Margrave Roland of Brittany was attacked by Christian Basques of Gascony in Pass of Roncesvalles. Roland killed; hero of many later songs and legends, notably famous *Chanson de Roland*.

3. Charles established East Spanish March, 793, comprising counties of Catalonia, Rousillon, and Barcelona. Another march created in western Pyrenees in 806.

   (a) The two joined together to form the Spanish March, 812.

   (1) Buffer territory against Islam.

   (2) The beginnings of Christian reconquest of Spain.

g. Charles and the Slavs and Avars.

1. Taught Slavic tribes dwelling beyond Elbe and in Bohemia to know and respect his power.

2. Conducted six campaigns (788-805) against Avars. Created Bavarian East March, the origin of Austria, 803.

3. His eastern frontier, girded with marches, was roughly the Elbe and Thuringian Saale rivers, the Bohemian forest, then south to the Adriatic.

V. CORONATION OF CHARLEMAGNE IN 800

a. Position and achievements of Charles.

1. He ruled all western territory of old Roman Empire save Africa, south Italy, Britain, and most of Spain; also German territory never subjugated by Rome.

2. Close, devoted, orthodox ally of Roman Church; Patrician of Rome and defender of Pope.

b. Position of Pope.

1. Roman populace ever turbulent; papal elections often caused violent factional quarrels; strong imperial authority needed.

Leo III in 799 assaulted by enemies; fled to Charles for protection.

   2. Roman Church preserved strong imperial tradition.
      (a) Constantinople weakened and tainted with heresy;
          Irene, a woman, reigned there.
      (b) Hence strong disposition at Rome to hail the
          orthodox and powerful Charles as Emperor.
  c. Charles surprised by papal coronation in Rome,
     Christmas day, 800.
     1. Even dismayed; reasons conjectural.
        (a) Not averse to dignity, but probably disliked idea
            of pope presuming to grant crown.
            (1) An unprecedented and illegal act.
            (2) See below under donation of Constantine.
  d. From this event dates the history of the medieval
     Roman Empire, later called Holy Roman Empire.

VI. SOME FEATURES OF CHARLEMAGNE'S SYSTEM

  a. His government machinery a continuation of Mero-
     vingian system, with some innovations.
     1. Chief of these the naming of *Missi Dominici* as im-
        perial circuit officials to control counts.
        Performed both ecclesiastical and secular work of super-
        vision and correction.
     2. Required all subjects to swear oath of allegiance to
        himself and of obedience to Church.
  b. The Church freely used as machinery of government.
     1. Charles disposed of its offices and lands as though they
        were his own.
     2. His great devotion to orthodoxy and religious interests
        made possible a policy which Popes were to deny to
        other Emperors.
  c. The military power.
     1. Constant activity of Charles and his soldiers necessary
        to maintain integrity of Empire.
     2. Universal obligation to bear arms on all free men.
        (a) Major burden was carried by Franks although
            Charles made military levies on his subject nations.
        (b) Service was limited to holders of three or more
            manors, 807.
     3. Growth of feudalism gradually diminished number of
        Franks available for military service.
  d. Legislation through capitularies.
     National codes of subject peoples respected.

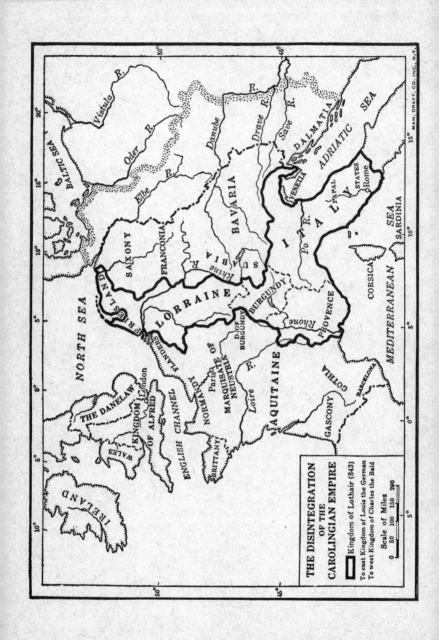

THE DISINTEGRATION
OF THE
CAROLINGIAN EMPIRE

■ Kingdom of Lothair (843)

To east Kingdom of Louis the German
To west Kingdom of Charles the Bald

Scale of Miles
0 50 100 150 200

e. Costs of government maintained chiefly from same sources of revenue upon which Merovingian rulers had drawn.

f. Empire of Charlemagne simply a crude military organization of Europe inspired by surviving Roman imperial ideal.

VII. SIGNIFICANCE OF CHARLES AND HIS AGE IN EUROPEAN CIVILIZATION

a. The culmination of Frankish political work.
   1. Stayed for a time the barbarian invasions.
   2. Provided opportunity for some recuperation of civilized life.

b. New life given to imperial tradition.

c. Charles energetically promoted civilized arts.
   1. Deeply interested in education; gathered about himself eminent scholars; zealously promoted schools.
   2. Historians have thus written of a *Carolingian Renaissance* of classic learning which helped to graft ancient civilization upon Germans.

d. Great widening of area of Christianity.

e. Charles' reign later was looked back upon as a golden age; he himself the heroic inspiration of much medieval romance and legend.

VIII. NINTH CENTURY CAROLINGIAN DISINTEGRATION

a. Frankish custom of partitioning kingdom among heirs was important factor in disintegration.
   1. Charles himself had no intention of departing from this; but only one son, Louis the Pious, survived him. This temporarily postponed the break-up.

b. Reign of Louis I, the Pious, 814-840.
   1. Less vigorous than father.
   2. Preparing for death or retirement, he partitioned realm among his three sons: Lothair, Pepin, and Louis (the German), 817. But Lothair was designated Emperor and placed over brothers.
   3. Fourth son, Charles the Bald (by Louis' second wife), necessitated new plan of division.
      Dreary succession of wars followed, brothers against one another and against father. In midst of these Pepin died, 838, and also Emperor Louis, 840.

c. Treaty of Verdun, 843.

1. War continued until Louis the German and Charles the Bald brought Lothair to terms at Verdun, 843.
2. Charles received western part, West Frankish Kingdom, in time to be called France.
3. Louis the German received lands east of Rhine, East Frankish Kingdom, the later Kingdom of Germany.
4. Lothair held middle kingdom stretching from Netherlands south through Rhineland, Meuse and Moselle valleys, to include Burgundy; also Lombard kingdom.

d. Further divisions and steady disintegration in second half ninth century.
1. Continued family rivalries and feuds.
2. New barbarian invasions.
3. Triumph of political feudalism.
4. Western Europe moved into so-called "Dark Ages."

Chapter IX

DESCENT OF THE NORTHERN AND OTHER INVADERS

I. NORTHMEN, WHO AND WHAT THEY WERE
a. Teutonic ancestors of modern Danes, Swedes, Norwegians.
1. Inhabitants of Scandinavian peninsula.
2. Racially akin to Germans; institutions very like those of primitive Germans already described.
b. Until eighth century lived in complete isolation from Roman civilization and Christianity.
c. Maritime fishing people, warlike, adventurous.
d. Their history before they were included in pale of Latin-Christian civilization is very obscure.

II. FAR-FLUNG MIGRATIONS OF THE NORTHMEN
a. Extended to Orkney, Faroe, and Shetland Islands, Iceland, Greenland, Ireland, England, France, Holland, Spain, Italy, Finland and northern Russia, Novgorod, Kiev, Constantinople.
b. Causes of migrations.
1. Pressure of population on subsistence.
2. Adventure, ambition, trade, piracy.

    3. Growth of social and economic inequality at home.

    4. Rise of national monarchies which were intolerable to freedom-loving *jarls*.

  c. Chief routes of the movement.

    1. Swedes struck across Baltic into Slavic Russia.

    2. Danes fell upon Western Europe and British Isles.

    3. Norwegians, with some Danes, moved upon Orkney, Faroe, and Shetland Islands, Iceland and Greenland.

III. DESCENT UPON CAROLINGIAN LANDS

  a. First attacks at close of eighth century.

  b. Annual and chronic by 850.

    1. Later Carolingians paid them tribute.

    2. West Frankish Kingdom suffered more than East.

  c. Only large-scale permanent settlement made in Seine valley.

    1. Leader of Northmen here was Rollo, who made Rouen his capital.

    This region was definitely granted to him in 911 by King Charles the Simple; so originated the Duchy of Normandy.

    2. Probably other smaller settlements of Northmen in Frankish lands.

    3. Everywhere they quickly were absorbed into Latin-Christian culture.

IV. DESCENT UPON BRITISH ISLES

  a. Attacks on Ireland.

    1. Began in 795 and became very serious by 823.

    Drove hundreds of Irish monks to refuge on European continent, notably Sedulius Scotus, the Irish poet, and John Scotus Erigena, the leading scholar of ninth century.

    2. Danes in 852 founded the "Kingdom of Dublin," which lasted nearly two hundred years.

  b. Attacks on England and Scotland also began before 800; in ninth century Danes occupied all northern and eastern England.

    1. Monastic culture virtually destroyed.

    2. Kingdoms of Mercia, Northumberland, East Anglia ended.

  c. King Alfred the Great.

    1. Gallant and noble Christian King of Wessex, 871-899, the leader of defense against Danes.

United rest of England against them

2. By Peace of Wedmore (879) Danes evacuated Wessex and accepted Christianity; seven years later boundary line made (roughly London to Liverpol) between Wessex and the *Danelagh*, or Danelaw.

d. Son and grandsons of Alfred gradually conquered Danelaw until by 954 all England was unified under rule of Wessex King, now rightly called King of England.

e. Another Danish invasion in eleventh century; Knut, son of King of Denmark and Norway, became King of England in 1016.

Dynasty lasted to 1042, when Wessex line was restored.

V. Iceland, Greenland, and Vinland

a. Voyages of Northmen to these distant lands illustrate well their hardy and adventuresome bravery.

b. Norwegians discovered Iceland about 861 and began its colonization in 874.

c. Erik the Red in 986 attempted to colonize Greenland. His son, Leif Erikson, continued the effort and also explored northwest coast of America (Vinland).

Greenland became established Norse colony, settled mostly from Iceland.

VI. Swedes in Russia

a. Recorded history of Russia begins with ninth century Swedish invasion.

1. Russia populated by Finnish and Slavic tribes; a commercial civilization had developed, chiefly along the great rivers.

2. Up the rivers came the Swedish plunderers, called *vaeringjar*, or Varangians; they lorded it over the native towns and tribes.

b. One Swedish chieftain, Rurik, got possession of Kiev about 882, founded Duchy of Kiev which extended its sway over much of great Russian plain.

This was the political beginning of Russia.

c. Northmen in Russia gradually became Slavized, and also Christianized.

Byzantine Christianity officially adopted, 988.

VII. Development of Monarchy and Christianity in Scandinavia

a. Christianity and Kingship developed in Denmark soon after Frankish conquest of Saxony.

1. St. Ansgar, missionary monk, preached in Denmark from 826 to 861; conversion of country achieved by *c.* 1000.

2. Danish monarchy well established by eleventh century. King Knut, conqueror of England, a great and powerful monarch, ruling also Denmark, part of Scotland, Norway, and Pomeranian coast of Baltic.

b. But the first Scandinavian state of large dimensions was the Norwegian Kingdom established by Harold Fair-hair in 872.

1. Upon his death in 933 much war and confusion followed, which ended in Danes becoming masters of Norway.

2. King Olaf I (995-1000) actively promoted spread of Christianity through Scandinavian peninsula.

c. Beginnings of monarchy in Sweden also in ninth-tenth centuries; Christianity there had made great headway by 1000.

VIII. Great Historic Importance of Northmen

a. Although they were disruptive of Frankish Empire and western Christian civilization, they brought vast new stores of energy into European world.

1. Displayed great capacity for adapting themselves to culture of countries in which they settled, for disseminating that culture.

b. Normans became leaders in feudal society; soon exhibited remarkable capacity for governing.

c. Their enterprising, adventurous impulse continued to show itself in eleventh and twelfth centuries in:

1. Upbuilding of Duchy of Normandy.
2. Conquest of England by Normans, 1066.
3. Creation of Norman Kingdom of Sicily and southern Italy.
4. Great crusading activity.

IX. Saracen Invasions of Sicily and Southern Italy

a. Moslems raided in the south, simultaneously with Norman onslaughts.

    b. Progressive Moslem domination of Sicily (until then Byzantine), 827-902.

    c. Naples in 837 called on Saracens for aid against Duke of Beneventum; soon followed overrunning of Byzantine Italy.

      1. Suburbs of Rome plundered, 846.

      2. Emperor Louis II, 855-875, led unsuccessful expeditions to expel them (part of the time in coöperation with Byzantines).

      3. Finally driven out by Pope John X in 915; but their possession of Sicily endured to eleventh century.

X. MAGYAR OR HUNGARIAN INVASION

    a. New wave of mounted Asiatic nomads, Magyars, appeared upon plains of Hungary and middle Danube, late ninth century.

Threatened conquest of Germany; also ravaged Gaul and Lombardy.

    b. Not until restoration of German monarchical power under Henry I and Otto I was the menace reduced.

    c. Magyars established permanent kingdom in Hungary and were converted to Christianity under King Stephen, 997-1038.

XI. SLAVIC WORLD OF NINTH AND TENTH CENTURIES

    a. Slavs of central Europe in second half ninth century gradually shook free from Carolingian influence.

      1. Tribal dynasties began to emerge.

      2. Incursions across Elbe into Germany.

      3. Temporary "Empire" of the Moravians under Svatopluk arose at the close of ninth century.

    b. The Magyar invasion drove wedge between Slavs north and south of Danube.

      1. Those to north, Wends, Poles, Bohemians, etc., were checked by rise of German monarchy in tenth century; and gradually Christianized by Latin Church.

      2. Those to south very largely dominated in tenth century by Asiatic Bulgarians; gradually Christianized by Greek Church.

Chapter X

THE PAPACY, THE CHURCH, AND THE SAXON REVIVAL OF THE EMPIRE

I. **Eminent Position of the Pope by the Ninth Century**

   a. Is well demonstrated by coronation of Charlemagne.

     1. Spiritual supremacy acknowledged throughout west.

   b. The donation of Constantine.

     1. Much legend had become clustered about the benefactions of Constantine I to the Church.

     2. Anonymous document appeared in eighth century to show that Constantine had abdicated imperial prerogatives and properties in the west in favor of Roman bishop.

      This was exploited to establish papal leadership and right of dispensing imperial crown.

   c. The notable pontificate of Nicholas I, 858-867.

     1. Vigorously interfered in quarrel between rivals for see of Constantinople.

     2. Coerced the ambitious and refractory Archbishop Hincmar of Rheims.

     3. Sternly disciplined the Carolingian prince, King Lothair of Lotharingia, for moral delinquencies.

     4. Established new precedents for energetic correction of abuses and misdeeds throughout Christendom.

   d. The Pseudo-Isadorean Decretals.

     1. Anonymous appearance in ninth century of spurious documents, supposedly letters and canons from early popes and councils.

     (a) Manufactured precedents for dealing with ninth century problems. They made for:

       (1) Freedom of church from lay control.

       (2) Supremacy of pope over episcopacy.

     2. Almost universally accepted as genuine; today no one defends them.

II. **Sorry Plight of the Church and Degradation of the Papacy at the Close of Ninth Century**

   a. Triumph of political anarchy and feudalism in later Carolingian times had ruinous consequences for Church.

     1. Lands despoiled by rapacious feudality, and Northmen, Saracens, and Hungarians.

      2. Bishops and abbots in self-defense joined the warrior caste.

      Whole ecclesiastical system drawn into feudalism and brought under lay domination.

  b. Position of Papacy illustrates well these dark ages for Christianity.

      1. Decline of imperial authority in Italy made papal lands prey for lawless elements.

      2. Papacy became militarized to defend its own and ward off Saracens in southern Italy.

      3. Rome disorderly and violent; Papacy dragged into local politics, and became the prize over which the most disreputable factions struggled.

      4. Scandalous situation not materially improved until the vigorous revival of imperial interference at Rome by Otto I.

  c. The seed of reform at work even at darkest hour.

III. RISE OF THE SAXON MONARCHY IN GERMANY

  a. Kingdom of East Franks (Germany) held together in ninth century disorders better than other Carolingian lands.

      1. Louis the German the ablest son of Louis the Pious; reigned to 876.

      2. Another able King was Arnulf, whose enthronement followed deposition of Charles the Fat in 887.

      3. But kingdom split apart into great tribal duchies during reign of Arnulf's son, Louis the Child, 898-911.

      Saxony, Bavaria, Suabia, Franconia, Lorraine, each with its own ducal government.

  b. German nobles in 919 chose as king Henry the Fowler, Duke of Saxony.

      1. Strongest of the dukes.

      2. Provided successful defense against Slavs and Magyars.

      3. Content to lead rather than govern Germany. Yet supplied a leadership that paved way for strong monarchy of his son, Otto I.

      4. Henry I suspicious of ecclesiastical politics.

  c. Reign of Otto I, 936-973.

      1. Humbled or dethroned other dukes, utilized Church as instrument of royal polity, established centralized monarchy, asserted German power against Slavs and Hungarians.

      2. Made Germany a great and strong monarchy in sharp

contrast with feudal disintegration of rest of Christendom.

d. Politico-ecclesiastical character of Saxon monarchy.

1. Otto's power really built upon Church, raised up as counterpoise against upper feudality.

2. His policy was twofold:

    (a) Enriching Church, thus making it socially and economically powerful.

    (b) Controlling it by filling bishoprics with his trusted lieutenants.

3. Success of policy due to:

    (a) Superiority of churchmen of that age in intelligence and ability.

    (b) No danger that offices would become hereditary and escape the appointing power of crown.

4. Momentous consequences of policy.

    (a) Raised German episcopacy to enormous temporal wealth and authority.

    (b) Probably reduced their spiritual authority.

    (c) Endangered the very life of the monarchy when, in eleventh century, arose the reform movement which aimed at removing church from all secular control.

IV. OTTO ACQUIRES ITALY AND THE EMPIRE

a. First descent upon Italy, 951.

Acquired rights and ambitions in Italy by intervening in Lombard quarrel against Berengar and marriage with Queen Adelheid.

b. In 962 went to Rome and received crown of Empire.

1. Otto's coronation does not mark founding of a new Empire; it was regarded as the same power that had survived from antiquity; after this it is usually called the Holy Roman Empire.

2. Otto's system in Italy fundamentally like that in Germany: patronage and political exploitation of Church.

c. Next few years Otto spent fighting in south Italy.

1. Byzantine Emperor had refused recognition of Otto's imperial title.

2. Otto failed to acquire lower Italy, but did succeed in marrying his son to Byzantine princess, Theophano.

V. EMPERORS OTTO II, OTTO III, AND HENRY I

a. Italy and imperial traditions exercised strong appeal to Otto and his successors.

b. The reign of Otto II, 973-983.
1. Suppression of Bavarian revolt
2. Attempted invasion of France.
3. Crowned Emperor at Rome, 981; suppressed the government which Crescentius, a Roman noble, had set up there in the imperial absence.
4. Died in Rome while organizing a campaign against Saracens.

c. Reign of Otto III, 983-1002.
1. A mere child; his mother, Theophano, regent until 996; educated by leading scholar of day, Gerbert of Aurillac, afterwards Pope.
2. A son of imperial house of east and west; very much under spell of Roman imperial tradition; died at twenty-three in 1002.

d. Reign of Henry II.
1. German crown passed to Henry of Bavaria, collateral Saxon line.
2. Gave energetic attention to German affairs but also felt lure of Imperial Italy.

VI. GERMANIC CONTROL OF THE PAPACY
  a. Otto I insisted no Pope should be consecrated without taking oath of fealty to Emperor.
  b. Otto I deposed Pope John XII in 963 for conspiring against him, and appointed a new Pope, Leo VIII.
  c. Practices of Otto I continued by successors.
1. Otto III 996 elevated a German to Papacy, Gregory V.
2. Otto III made his former tutor Gerbert (another German) Pope in 999: Sylvester II.
3. Some relaxation of German influence at Rome under Henry II.
  d. Bitter Roman resentment at Germanic dictation.

CHAPTER XI

FEUDALISM

I. MEANING AND NATURE OF FEUDALISM
  a. Refers to a kind of political organization and structure of society which took form in medieval Europe and was at its height from the age of Carolingian dissolution down to thirteenth century.

1. In strict sense feudalism denotes network of relationships which bound together members of the military and landlord class.
2. In broad sense it denotes the whole political, social, and economic life of those times.

b. Feudalism politically considered.

1. Absence of strong central governments and concept of the abstract principle of the state.
2. Political order maintained by series of contractual relationships between men.
   (a) This contract based on land tenure.
   (b) No separation between public authority and private ownership, or between government and proprietorship.

c. Feudalism as social structure.

1. Feudal society pyramidal in structure, every man being subordinated to another; structure derives from land tenure, since each man holds land as vassal of another.
2. The pyramid is composed of the dominant social class: military and ecclesiastical land-holding aristocracy.
3. Pyramid rests on great mass of servile peasants, who are outside of contractual system.

II. EVOLUTION OF FEUDALISM

a. Conditions giving rise to it.

1. Disorder and insecurity prevalent after Germanic irruption into Roman world.
   Combated with partial success by barbarian monarchies; but dissolution of Carolingian Empire gave full reign for long period to forces of anarchy.
2. In time of political and social anarchy the individual, lacking protection of state, seeks protection elsewhere. Weaker men take refuge under the stronger men who by virtue of wealth, position, and ability can give protection.

b. Feudal tendencies in later Roman Empire.

1. Landed aristocracy took over many rights of local administration.
2. Dependent land tenure widely developed; many surviving small holders surrendered up lands to large and powerful proprietors, receiving them back again to cultivate as tenants under the *precarium* lease.
   (a) A lease recognized by Roman law whereby owner

granted use of property to another without rent and on no contractual terms.

A refuge for small owners harassed by taxes, brigands, barbarian invaders; they found protection while losing independent proprietorship.

(b) This enormously increased the influence of the great proprietors.

3. Common practice for impoverished freemen to place themselves in service and under patronage of rich and powerful men; received shelter and support and gave such services as freemen might becomingly perform. This patronage known as the *patrocinium*.

Out of the *patrocinium* arose considerable private armies in age of invasions.

4. These feudal tendencies underwent modification and fused with others introduced by German invaders to create feudal politics and society.

c. Some Germanic factors.

1. Germanic kings and chieftains, coming into Roman world, seized lands and parcelled out grants.

Had little conception of absolute property in land; tenure of grants generally dependent on loyalty of service.

2. Another Germanic element was the *comitatus*.

(a) Person to person relationship, somewhat like Roman *patrocinium*; fighting, aristocratic thanes recognized their highest loyalty in obligation to chieftain.

d. Commendation

1. In sixth century arose practice for lesser men to obtain protection of greater men by *commending* themselves to the latter, i.e., agreeing to perform certain services (and usually hand over lands) in return for protection and tenancy.

2. This did not necessarily carry any degradation.

3. Led directly to the lord-vassal bond of feudalism.

e. The *beneficium*, or benefice.

1. This was the land element engaged in the transaction of *commendation*.

2. It was a grant of land made by one proprietor to another lesser proprietor, or to any freeman, who took oath of fidelity therefor.

3. Grant was conditional, and definition of the conditions was evolved by custom and practice.

4. It was very common for men, wishing to make benefactions to the Church, to hand over property to some abbey and then receive it back again as a benefice for remainder of their lives.

5. Charles Martel influenced most importantly the system of benefice-holding by seizing church lands and distributing them among select nobles as benefices, the tenure of which depended upon military service to Frankish leader.

6. Charlemagne greatly extended the practice of beneficed lands.

f. Much of the history of the evolution of feudalism is obscure and controversial, but it is certain that by the ninth century the above factors had contributed importantly to an economic system of dependent land tenure, a social system of personal dependence, and a political system in which the duties men owed to the crown sprang largely from their position as tenants of estates held from the crown.

g. <u>Disintegration of Frankish Empire</u>.

1. Benefice-holders made tenures hereditary.

2. Territorial nobles and crown officials converted estates and powers into private political jurisdictions.

3. Nobles constructed castles to protect themselves and those who had made commendations.

4. Hierarchy of vassalage and suzerainship arose as state vanished and gates of anarchy opened.

h. <u>Warrior aristocracy now independent lords, only nominally subservient to crown.</u>

1. Each had his own group of vassals.

2. The word benefice replaced by fief (feodum); subject to satisfactory discharge of feudal obligations, it was now a hereditary tenure.

i. Although characteristic features of European feudalism appeared first in Frankish Gaul, by eleventh century feudal régime obtained, in varying form, throughout Europe.

III. Characteristic Feudal Customs and Institutions

a. <u>The feudal contract entered into by act of fealty.</u>

1. Vassal did homage: took oath to become the lord's man, or vassal, all the days of his life.

    2. Followed investiture of fief by some symbolic act, e.g., stroke with little rod, or handing clod of earth.

b. <u>The usual duties of vassalage.</u>

    1. Performance of military service.
- (a) At vassal's own expense.
- (b) With required number of retainers.
- (c) Custom limited term of service to forty days **per** year.
- (d) In time this obligation often was converted to cash payment (scutage), which enabled lords to hire mercenaries who would fight as long as they were paid.

    2. Civil obligation.
- (a) To attend lord's court and assist him in establishing justice.
- (b) To plead his own case in lord's court and assist him in hearing others, either in capacity of juror or associate judge.

    3. Financial obligations.
- (a) Payment of feudal dues, or aids.
  - (1) For ransom, if lord was captured in war.
  - (2) At knighting of lord's eldest son.
  - (3) At marriage of lord's eldest daughter.
- (b) Payment of feudal relief.
  Sum exacted whenever the personal contract was renewed.
- (c) Purveyance, or provision of hospitality to lord.

c. <u>The customary rights of suzerainship</u> (deriving from obligation to protect vassal).

    1. Benefit of vassal's duties as outlined above.

    2. Right to administer justice.
- (a) Greater nobles possessed "high" justice, or right to inflict capital punishment.
- (b) Lesser lords had "mean," or "low" justice: correction by lesser punishments.

    3. Right of wardship: guardianship of vassal during latter's minority and enjoyment of usufruct of fief.

    4. Right of escheat: reversion of vassal's fief when vassal died without heir.

    5. Right of forfeiture: confiscation of fief for cause.

    6. Right to control marriage of vassal's children.

IV. FEUDAL WARFARE

a. Continuous private warfare the greatest evil of feudalism.

The military tradition of the dominant class viewed war as the major aristocratic occupation; and besides, the very nature of feudal organization bred a ceaseless collision of interests and loyalties.

b. The Church succeeded in greatly moderating warfare.

1. Local synods in southern France, 989, 990, 994, proclaimed the Peace of God, threatening with ecclesiastical anathema all who plundered church lands, peasants, women, children, and merchants. This spread over most of France.

2. By Truce of God (mid-eleventh century) Church forbade, under pain of excommunication, fighting on Fridays, Saturdays, and Sundays; later long periods of calendar were declared peace periods.

V. CHIVALRY, THE FLOWER OF FEUDAL CIVILIZATION

a. Splendid and honorable order of chivalry arose in the twelfth and thirteenth century out of the wreckage of European society, militarized and barbarized.

b. The word meant originally nothing more than mounted soldiery; but it came to mean a social order wedded to ideals of honor, heroism, and courtesy.

1. Major influences giving rise to chivalry:

   (a) Military traditions of aristocracy.

   (b) Encouragement of kings, who, in breaking up political independence of feudality, encouraged preservation of its honors and social privileges.

   (c) Christian idealism and the crusades.

c. The military class of feudal Europe gradually evolved a polite aristocracy throughout Christendom.

1. Although every noble was not a knight, every knight was a noble.

2. Until thirteenth century chivalry was an order into which men of non-noble birth often made their way through service and valor.

3. The fashion among noble families to place sons under knights for training in courtesy, deportment, and chivalric ideals.

d. Church grafted Christian ideals upon those of the refined and courteous warrior.

1. Defined the mission of the knight: defense of Church, protection of poor, redress of wrongs.

    2. Initiation into knighthood made a religious ritual; St. Mary the Virgin became patron of every knight, and she represented the loftiest ideal of woman.

  e. Chivalry flourished at height in thirteenth century; then greatly degenerated into arrogant, reactionary caste.

VI. PEASANTRY AND THE MANORIAL SYSTEM

  a. Three classes, or *estates,* in feudal society: clergy, nobility, peasantry.

    1. First two were privileged; their functions were to minister to religious needs, govern and protect.

    2. The third class had duty of working for material support of whole of society.

  b. The servile population.

    1. Peasantry nearly everywhere composed of serfs. Varying gradations of servitude.

    2. Descended from Roman coloni and slaves, unfree Germans of age of invasions, and freemen whose condition was depressed in the evolution of feudalism.

    3. Dwelt in small village communities on manors of nobles and Church; a manor was an agricultural estate. This known as manorial system.

  c. Manorialism was economic and social, but not political; to be carefully distinguished from feudalism. Manorialism was the relation of landed proprietors to their servile tenantry, whereas feudalism was an honorable contractual relation between privileged nobles and churchmen.

CHAPTER XII

THE EMPIRE AND THE PAPACY TO 1183

I. HOLY ROMAN EMPIRE AND HOLY ROMAN CHURCH

  a. Minds of medieval men held by two universal ideas:

    1. The imperial tradition.

    2. The idea of Christendom.

  b. There seemed a permanent, divine plan for organization of human society: Empire and Church, with head of each viewed as God's vicar.

c. Theoretical harmony between the two:
  1. Emperor ruled in matters temporal, Pope in spiritual.
  2. But in practice much discord; no clear line of demarcation between jurisdictions.

II. SECULAR DOMINATION OF CHURCH
  a. Down to eleventh century, throughout Christendom, Church affairs very much under control of lay powers.
    1. This control carried to high point in time of Charlemagne.
    2. After Charlemagne Church fell to a great extent under the tyranny and lawless domination of feudality.
    3. The new Saxon monarchy in Germany and Italy revived and greatly extended the policy of Charlemagne. Brought whole ecclesiastical system of Empire under iron-handed imperial control.
  b. Lay investiture.
    1. The practice of secular princes in nominating Church officials.
    2. In Holy Roman Empire bishops and abbots held feudal lands as fiefs of crown, and were nominated by the crown. The very offices of Church came to be regarded also as fiefs of crown.
      (a) In eleventh century Emperors developed famous ring and staff investiture of bishops.

III. RISE OF THE CLUNIAC REFORM
  a. Sorry plight of Church in tenth century; led to reform movements, originating in monastic circles. Greatest of these was the Cluniac movement.
  b. Origin of Cluny.
    1. William the Pious, Duke of Aquitaine, granted to one Berno a freehold in Burgundy; abbey founded, 910.
    2. William placed it directly under papal authority; so that it was from the start exempt from near-by episcopal control; also, it stood outside the system of dependent feudal land tenure.
    3. Long line of able abbots, under whom it became shining example of righteous and ascetic monastic life.
  c. The congregational Order of Cluny.
    1. Endowments multiplied and more asked to join the

cloister than could be received; so that other cloisters were founded or taken over.

   2. Over each monastery affiliated with Cluny was placed a prior subject to the Abbot at Cluny.

      Thus arose, instead of the Benedictine system of independent abbeys, the centralized Order of Cluny.

   3. Order spread through much of Christendom and became very powerful; the vanguard of reform.

  d. The reform program, in eleventh century, broadened out from previous concern only with monastic life to demand for:

   1. Extension of celibacy to secular clergy.

    (a) Hitherto Church had not imposed rule of celibacy on priesthood, and many were quite lawfully married.

    (b) The danger perceived was that the hereditary tendency in feudalism was threatening to make clergy a hereditary caste.

   2. Suppression of lay investiture.

    (a) To release Church from feudal tyranny.

    (b) The system bred *simony*, or trafficking in Church offices.

    (c) Radical Cluniacs attacked all lay control of Church as simoniacal.

   3. A third very important part of Cluniac reform was the strengthening of papal supremacy.

IV. GERMAN AFFAIRS IN ELEVENTH CENTURY (TO 1075)

  a. The feud between the bishops and the monks.

   1. Saxon dynasty had greatly promoted episcopal power, even at expense of monasteries.

    (a) Henry II, 1002-1024, piously sympathetic with purification and improvement of monastic life, strengthened episcopal control of it and stripped abbeys of property.

    (b) Aroused bitter opposition from monks and inclined them toward Cluniac doctrines.

   2. Royal election of 1024 very much a struggle between bishops and abbots, with former triumphing in choice of Conrad II, 1024-1039, the first of the Salian dynasty.

  b. Conrad II's modification of Saxon system.

   1. Although reposing his power mainly on bishops, he began new and significant policy.

      (a) Favoring lesser feudality as counterpoise to both bishops and higher lay feudality.

      (b) Also using *ministeriales:* men of servile origin taken into service of crown.

    2. Crown authority in Germany greatly strengthened.

    3. Feudal Kingdom of Burgundy added to Empire, 1033.

  c. The reign of Henry III, 1039-1056.

    1. German monarchical power stronger than it had yet been; he was most powerful of all medieval emperors.

      (a) Vigorously asserted German power in Bohemia, Hungary, and Italy.

      (b) But there was ominous growth of disaffection in Saxony.

    2. King sympathetic to Cluniac reform, without fully realizing its ultimate political consequences.

      (a) Benevolent attitude toward monasteries.

      (b) Interfered at Rome to put a reform Pope, Leo IX, on throne (1049-1054).

  d. The reign of Henry IV to 1075.

    1. A child king under regency of mother, Empress Agnes.

    2. General feudal reaction.

    3. Formidable revolt of Saxony, 1070 ff.

    4. Henry fought his way through to victory.

    In doing so laid heavy hand on Church, and Pope in 1075 opened the famous struggle with him.

V. ITALIAN AND PAPAL AFFAIRS TO 1075

  a. Bitter hostility in Italy toward Germanic rule, which was chiefly sustained by German bishops.

  b. Italians saw supreme political advantage in Cluny reform; took up agitation against lay investiture.

  Rise of Pataria in eleventh century; center at Milan; religious, semi-national, anti-German movement; inveighed against German hierarchy.

  c. The Papacy and the Cluniac movement.

    1. Papacy slow in taking up Cluniac reform.

      (a) Popes were not very remarkable men, 1003-1049. Recurrence of scandalous conditions at Rome.

      (b) Serious papal scandal in 1046: three claimants to papal throne.

      Henry III vigorously interfered, reviving strong imperial influence at Rome, and placed on throne

Leo IX, the German Bishop of Toul. On his death another German, Victor II, was elevated in 1054.

2. Pontificate of Leo IX.

   (a) This Pope an earnest reformer, but not a radical Cluniac.

   (b) Party at papal court, led by Hildebrand, radically Cluniac, grew in influence.

3. Towards the great revolution, 1056 to 1073.

   (a) Sudden lapse of imperial influence at Rome with death of Henry III, 1056.

   (b) Anti-imperialist, Stephen X, consecrated, 1057.

      (1) Nourished ardent desire for reform and ecclesiastical liberty.

      (2) Hildebrand at this time went to Milan and drew Pataria closer to Papacy.

   (c) Nicholas II (1059-1061) chosen and consecrated by Hildebrandine party.

      (1) Procedure of papal elections reformed by College of Cardinals decree (1059); struck veiled blow at imperial influence in papal elections.

      (2) Papacy drew closer to new Norman power in South Italy (see below d.).

   (d) Alexander II, 1061-1073, strongly Hildebrandine. German and Lombard bishops refused recognition and set up anti-Pope; long conflict ensued; grave disorders throughout the Empire.

4. Hildebrand elected Pope as Gregory VII, 1073.

   (a) Had very exalted conception of papal powers and prerogatives (note the famous Dictatus); radical Cluniac bent on securing freedom of Church regardless of consequences to Empire.

   (b) In 1075 he precipitated revolution.

d. The rise of the Norman power in south Italy.

1. Southern Italy in early eleventh century scene of great anarchy, into which came Norman adventurers, 1016 ff.

   (a) Band of them appeared at Aversa c. 1030; increased and became formidable military power.

      (1) Notable were the eight sons of Tancred of Hauteville, the chief of whom was Robert Giuscard (1015?-1085).

      (2) Dominated virtually all of southern Lombard and Byzantine Italy by mid-eleventh century.

   (b) Robert Giuscard became Pope's vassal (1059) and held his conquests as papal fiefs.

So began papal suzerainship over the power that was to become Kingdom of Naples.

2. Robert Giuscard and vassals fought cause of western orthodoxy against Byzantine schismatics, and gave strong aid to Gregory VII in struggle with imperial power.

VI. Investitures War, 1075-1122

a. Gregory VII's revolutionary decrees of 1075.

1. Rule of celibacy for all secular clergy.
2. Renewed prohibition of simony.
3. Absolute prohibition of lay investiture.
   (a) Directed specially against Henry IV of Germany.
   (b) This struck at root of imperial monarchy; almost a demand for abdication.

b. Henry, who had just vindicated his authority in Saxony, paid no immediate attention to papal decrees; Gregory (Jan. 2, 1076) sent him a sharp reprimand.

1. Henry, full of indignation, summoned council at Worms (to which came two-thirds of bishops of Germany).
   Addressed letters to Gregory accusing him of being uncanonically elected and attempting to usurp unlawful powers.
2. Gregory replied by excommunicating Henry and decreeing his deposition as king.

c. Momentous consequences followed decree of deposition.

1. The bond of feudal society was snapped.
2. Henry forced to seek the Pope's pardon.
   Crossed Alps and sought out Pope (Feb. 1077), at Canossa; secured pardon at price of great humiliation.
3. Henry returned to Germany to fight for his authority.
   (a) Hostile nobles raised up Rudolf, Duke of Suabia, as anti-king; rebellion suppressed, 1080.
   (b) Ban of excommunication renewed.
4. Henry invaded Italy, 1081-1085; Gregory driven from Rome to die defeated at Salerno in 1085.

d. Collapse of Henry's fortunes, 1085-1106.

1. Upon return to Germany his enemies at Rome, supported by Normans, obtained power; succeeding Popes continued irreconcilable.

2. Great difficulty in maintaining peace and government in Germany and Lombardy.

    (a) Son Conrad revolted and put himself at head of Lombard opposition, 1093; by 1100 imperialist cause in Italy was ruined.

    (b) His son and heir (Henry V) led feudal revolt in Germany, (1104) which forced his abdication.

3. Henry died in 1106, defeated and excommunicated.

e. <u>Henry V, 1106-1125</u>, and resumption of struggle with Pope.

1. Immediately began filling vacant bishoprics without papal consent; threatened with ban.

2. Henry (1110) marched on Rome and forced terms on Pope.

    (a) First a compromise was reached: Church to surrender feudal lands and live on tithes and voluntary contributions, while Emperor gave up lay investiture. This broke down under clerical opposition.

    (b) Henry then by force extorted from Pope Pascal II an assent to the imperial demand for lay investiture, and retired to the north.

3. Pascal II repudiated agreement and put Henry under ban.

4. Followed protracted struggle throughout Empire until peace was achieved in 1122.

f. <u>The Concordat of Worms</u>, concluded between Emperor Henry V and Pope Calixtus II, 1122.

1. Distinguished between spiritual offices and temporal lands and functions attached to them.

    (a) Free canonical elections in Church.

    (b) Papal confirmation of elections.

    (c) Royal investiture only through the lance, i.e., only investiture of temporalities.

2. Crown control of Church not destroyed.

    (a) In Germany presence of crown necessary for valid election, so that crown could invalidate any ecclesiastical candidacy disapproved of by remaining absent; investiture of temporalities was to precede consecration, which further enabled crown to block candidacies.

    (b) In Italy and Burgundy no crown presence was necessary for canonical election, and investiture of temporalities was to follow consecration.

3. Essentially a compromise, with Pope winning a victory in principle but failing to emancipate Church from feudal domination.

g. Some important observations on the long struggle.

1. German feudality, especially the great ducal authorities, won a victory against the absolutist ambitions of the Salian imperial house.

2. Italy gained a large freedom from Germanic rule.

3. Investiture question settled as far as possible under the feudal order.

4. During the struggle a great opportunity was lost to Emperor when the first crusade was launched, 1095 ff. Pope captured European leadership in a great enterprise involving all Christendom.

5. Struggle stirred intellectual ferment; appeals to law and history; contributed importantly to revival of study of Roman law in Italy.

VII. GERMANY UNDER LOTHAIR AND THE FIRST HOHEN-STAUFEN, 1125-1152

a. Reign of Lothair II, 1125-1139.

1. Elected with party feelings running high.

2. Frederick and Conrad of Hohenstaufen, nephews of Henry V, refused to submit and were forcibly suppressed.

3. Lothair's principal supporter was Henry the Proud of Bavaria, of Guelf family, who later married Lothair's daughter and became his heir.

4. Lothair a clerical sympathizer; no disposition to reopen quarrel with Papacy.

(a) More interest in German conquest and colonization of Slavic lands east of Saxony; in his time a great movement was launched which led to German possession of Mecklenburg, Brandenburg, and Pomerania.

b. The reign of Conrad III, 1139-1152.

1. Contenders for crown in 1139 were Conrad of Hohenstaufen and Henry the Proud, Guelf duke of Bavaria and Saxony.

2. Guelfs and Ghibellines.

(a) Conrad sought to break feudal power of Henry; latter appealed to sword and was slain.

(b) Struggle continued in behalf of Henry's infant son, Henry the Lion, by his uncle, Welf (or Guelf); at siege of Weinsberg cries of warriors were for

"Welf" or "Waiblingen" (Suabian village where Conrad of Hohenstaufen was born). These became party names:

(1) Former the party of the great feudality.
(2) Latter the party that stood for strong monarchy.
(3) These names carried to Italy as Guelf and Ghibelline, where they denoted, roughly, 1. the party of the papacy and Italian local independence, and 2. the imperialist party.

3. Conrad took leading part in second crusade, 1147.
4. Just before death in 1152 recommended succession to his nephew, Frederick, and to him the sceptre passed.

c. <u>Frederick I (Barbarossa or the Red-beard), 1152-1189.</u>

1. Vigorous, young, and popular ruler.
2. Immediately sought to heal feud with Guelfs by promising reversion of Bavaria to Henry the Lion.
3. Germany at peace internally in early years; Frederick set off for Italy soon to gain the imperial crown. That was the prelude to long efforts to revive strong imperial dominion there.

VIII. <u>ITALY AND THE PAPACY BEFORE FREDERICK I</u>

a. Rise of flourishing town life in Lombard Italy.

1. Many towns asserted municipal independence from feudal and episcopal government.
2. Such a revolt took place against the Pope in Rome in 1144.
   Arnold of Brescia, a leading radical of the age, seized leadership; sought to end temporal power of Papacy and restore the ancient republican order in Rome.

b. The Papacy and the Normans.

1. Normans of south Italy went to war with their suzerain, the Pope, in 1127.
2. Duke Roger II forced a schism in Papacy in 1130, setting up own Pope who granted him title of king.
3. Emperor Lothair tried without success to punish Roger.
4. Continued bad blood between Norman Kingdom and Papacy.

c. Pope appealed to Frederick Barbarossa for aid.

IX. <u>FREDERICK BARBAROSSA'S STRUGGLE FOR ITALIAN DOMINION, 1154-1183</u>

a. <u>His first expedition, 1154-1155.</u>

1. Reduced to obedience several Lombard towns.

2. Suppressed Roman Republic and hanged Arnold of Brescia.

3. But returned to Germany without attacking Normans. Whereupon Pope Hadrian IV (1154-1159) entered entente with Normans, to Frederick's chagrin.

b. The Besançon Episode of 1157.

Pope addressed communication to Frederick at Besançon (Burgundy), seemingly taking the view that Frederick held the Empire as a fief of the Pope. Additional bad blood and distrust between Frederick and Hadrian.

c. Frederick's expedition of 1158.

1. Summoned Diet of Roncaglia, assemblage of deputies from Lombard towns.
There insisted on extensive imperial rights of government, supporting claims by appeal to the Roman law.

2. Over each city Frederick placed a podesta.

3. Cities resisted with papal encouragement (for Pope too was menaced by Frederick's ambitions) and bitter struggle ensued.

d. Frederick's additional expeditions.

1. Made upon subsequent occasions down to 1176.

2. The great issue was the proposed establishment of a powerful imperial absolutism, subversive of both local and papal independence.

3. Lombard League, formed in 1167 under patronage of Pope Alexander III (1159-1181), united most of Italy against its German suzerain.
League decisively victorious in Battle of Legnano, 1176.

e. Failure of imperialist aims.

1. Frederick made peace with Pope at Venice in 1177, acknowledging his independence and restoring disputed lands.

2. Frederick made peace at Constance with Italian towns in 1183; their liberties vindicated.

3. Great result of the Frederician attempt was to tear Holy Roman Empire south of Alps to shreds; feudal levies of Germany beaten by rising commercial and industrial cities of Italy.

X. FREDERICK I AND GERMANY; HIS LAST YEARS

a. Germany fairly well united during most of reign.

Warrior aristocracy busy fighting Slavs to the east, as well as Italians.

b. But Guelf-Hohenstaufen feud was torn open in 1176.

1. Henry the Lion, Frederick's most powerful and dangerous vassal, long disapproving Frederick's Italian policy and ambitions as wasteful to Germany, withdrew his support on eve of Legnano.

2. Frederick determined to punish him; moreover, German nobles and bishops, defeated in Italy, wanted compensation for losses.

3. Henry the Lion was broken and Saxony partitioned, 1181.
   Last of medieval German duchies to be sundered in feudal fragments.

c. Frederick closed his reign with appearance of triumph in Germany. Died on third crusade in 1190.

CHAPTER XIII

THE CRUSADES

I. MEANING OF THE CRUSADES AND THEIR MAJOR HISTORICAL PERIOD

a. Crusades were wars undertaken in behalf of religious objectives and approved by the Papacy.

1. But in addition to being great manifestations of popular religious zeal, they were adventurous migrations and forms of medieval economic expansion.

2. A phase of the long, historic conflict between Asia and Europe, East and West.

b. Period of most active crusading, 1095-1291.

1. But movement had its roots earlier and did not entirely cease until long afterwards.

2. Eight outstanding attacks on Moslem and eastern world may be distinguished in this period.

II. MOSLEM WORLD IN TENTH AND ELEVENTH CENTURIES

a. Political disintegration.

b. Christian counter-attacks on Islam began long before First Crusade.

1. Byzantine "Crusade," 961-975, resulted in recovery of Crete, Cyprus, and Syria.
2. Moslem retreat in Spain before expansion of Christian principalities in eleventh century.
3. Vigorous warfare of Italian city-states against Moslem sea power in Mediterranean.
4. Normans of South Italy conquered Sicily and Malta, 1060-1091.

c. Political revival in Moslem world began in several quarters not long before First Crusade.
1. Rise of Almoravide power in northwest Africa, c. 1050 ff; foundation of Moroccan Empire.
   Almoravides came to aid of retreating Moslems in Spain just as Alfonso VI of Castile was capturing Toledo (1085); followed temporary revival of Moslem power in Spain.
2. Advent of Seljuk Turks.
   (a) Came from Central Asia, embraced Islam, conquered Persia in tenth century, and in 1055 became masters of Bagdad. Caliph, in 1057, appointed Turkish Sultan to temporal rule over Moslem world; followed sweeping triumph of Turk arms throughout Western Asia.
   Turks were plunged into internal strife over succession to Sultanate, 1092 ff.

III. BYZANTINE EMPIRE BEFORE 1095

a. Had shown striking vitality and gone through several periods of great recuperative power down to eleventh century.
1. In spite of repeated attacks from barbarian and Moslem forces.
2. It remained the eastern outpost of Christendom against Moslem world and Asiatic barbarians.
3. Continued to enjoy richest commercial life in Christendom.
   This did not decline until the great swelling of direct Mediterranean trade between Italy and Levant.
4. Last notable period of Byzantine power and prosperity was reign of Basil II, 976-1025.

b. Byzantine misfortunes under Comneni dynasty.
1. Disintegrating feudal tendencies operating in Empire in eleventh century.

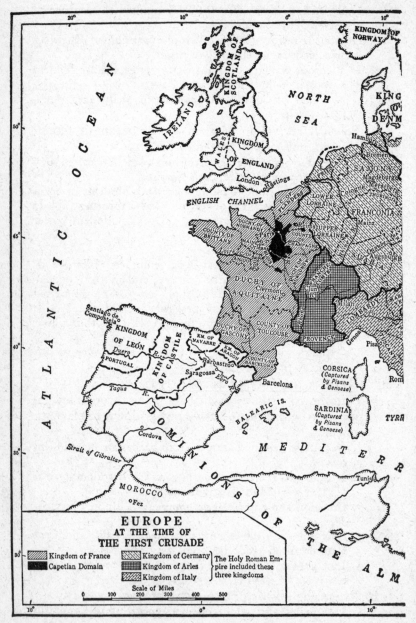

EUROPE
AT THE TIME OF
THE FIRST CRUSADE

Kingdom of France
Capetian Domain
Kingdom of Italy
Kingdom of Germany
Kingdom of Arles

The Holy Roman Empire included these three kingdoms

Scale of Miles
100   200   300   400   500

MAP X

2. Most influential element were the great landed proprietors, the *dunatoi,* of the Asiatic provinces.
   From them came the Emperor Isaac Comnenus, 1057-1059, founder of new dynasty.

3. Asiatic losses to Turks.
   Battle of Manzikert, 1071, tremendous defeat which opened up all Anatolian peninsula to Turkish conquest.

4. Strong rivalry between Normans of South Italy and Byzantine Empire.
   (a) Normans ended Greek rule in Italy by capture of Bari almost simultaneously with Manzikert.
   (b) Violent attacks on Byzantine power in Greek peninsula by Robert Giuscard, 1081-1085.

5. Constantinople also threatened from north by the Petchenegs.

6. Emperor Alexius Comnenus, 1081-1118, greatest of his dynasty, in very grave plight; but his position was temporarily improved by 1095 and he laid plans for recovery of Asiatic possessions.
   Sent appeal to Pope Urban II for aid of western knights against Turks.

c. The Schism between Greek and Latin Church.

1. Rupture came as result of long-standing differences.

2. Mutual excommunication between Rome and Constantinople occurred in 1054.

3. Wide hope that common enterprise against Turks would reunite Church.

IV. CAUSES FOR PRECIPITATION OF CRUSADES

a. Basic urge in western Europe caused by expanding population, a constant factor in feudal warfare.

b. Great love of warfare in feudal society combined with hereditary hatred for infidel and mighty religious fervor of eleventh century to give crusading a strong appeal.

c. Difficulties of Christian pilgrims and reports of atrocities in Near East.
   Under new Turkish domination serious obstacles were placed in way of pilgrimages to Holy Lands.

d. Exigencies of papal policy.

1. Christendom torn by struggle between temporal and spiritual authorities.

2. Call to crusade was a summons to unity, an appeal from turmoil at home to a common enemy.

e. Speech of Pope Urban II at Clermont (France), 1095.
1. Appealed to vast gathering of knights and clergy to take up cross and fight for recovery of Jerusalem.
2. Offered spiritual rewards: full remission of sins to all who went with pure hearts, without motive of gain.

f. Others took up task of preaching crusade and enormous enthusiasm fired west.
1. Essentially a popular movement; not only knights but people of all classes—even women and children—sought to go.
2. Chief figure in this was Peter the Hermit, monk of Amiens, who toured France on mule and organized a popular crusade.

V. FIRST CRUSADE AND ITS ACHIEVEMENTS
a. The "crusade" of Peter the Hermit and Walter the Penniless.
1. Illustrates the frenzied popular stampede; large bands (motley and nondescript), led by itinerant preachers, poured through central Europe to Constantinople.
2. Byzantines sent them across Bosphorus where they were almost all exterminated.

b. Knightly armies reached Constantinople in winter of 1096-1097.
1. Principal leaders: Godfrey de Bouillon, Count Robert of Flanders, Count Raymond of Toulouse, Count Baldwin of Flanders, and Bohemond (son of Robert Giuscard). Pope assumed general direction through legate.

c. Emperor Alexius and western knights.
1. Wished to turn expedition to political service of Byzantine Empire.
2. Alexius suspicious of rough visitors, especially of Bohemond and his Normans; fearful of assault on Constantinople.
3. Agreement made that conquered territory in Asia Minor should be restored to Alexius, who in turn would aid in the conquest of Jerusalem.

d. The descent upon Antioch.
1. Long and hazardous march through Asia Minor. Much dissension among leaders; Count Baldwin of

Flanders left main army and seized Edessa, there establishing first crusader principality.

2. Antioch captured, 1098; principality under Bohemond
instituted.

e. Capture of Jerusalem.

1. In dwindled numbers crusaders continued on to Jerusalem.

2. Holy City stormed and taken, July, 1099.

VI. LATIN KINGDOM OF JERUSALEM (1100-1291)

a. Organization of this was major political result of
First Crusade.

b. A feudal state of western design.

1. Comprised four great baronies: Edessa, Antioch, Trip-
oli, Jerusalem.   Each an almost independent unit.

2. Feudal land tenure and military system introduced.

3. Conscious importation made feudal institutions more
consistent, more nearly uniform, than anywhere else in
Christendom.

c. Ecclesiastical head of Kingdom was new Latin Patri-
arch of Jerusalem.

d. Subjection of coast towns.

1. Impossible without naval power.

2. Crusaders enlisted aid of Italian commercial city-states,
Genoa, Pisa, Venice, promising them booty and trade
privileges.   As a result Syrian ports fell to new Kingdom and its Italian allies.
So began Italian hold on Levant trade.

e. The Knights Templars and the Knights of the Hos-
pital of St. John of Jerusalem (latter came to be
called Knights of Malta).

1. These orders arose out of First Crusade.

2. Military-monastic in character; combinations of
chivalry and monasticism.

3. Assumed large share of defense of Kingdom and aiding
pilgrims to Holy Places.

4. Soon developed commanderies throughout Mediterranean.

5. Captured pious imagination of west and became richly
endowed.

6. They too acquired trading privileges and developed
business relations throughout west and in Levant.

f. Some weaknesses of the Kingdom of Jerusalem.

1. Its feudal constitution: great lords prone to intrigue against one another, even in alliance with Moslem chieftains and Byzantine Greeks.
2. Rivalry of military orders and commercial jealousy of Italian city-states.
3. Greek Byzantines very unreliable allies.
4. Oriental environment weakened religious ardor for fighting infidel; much intermarriage with natives and even some apostasy to Islam.
5. Many crusaders returned home and in order to sustain the Kingdom it was necessary to yield more and more to feudal ambition and Italian commercialism.
6. Safety of the principalities depended very largely upon disunity of Moslems.

VII. SECOND AND THIRD CRUSADES

a. The Emir (governor) of Mosul, Zenghi, an able Moslem chieftain, began new unification movement among Mohammedans of Mesopotamia in 1144. He captured Edessa and struck down Latin Christian authority east of Euphrates; this occasioned Second Crusade.

b. Preached by St. Bernard of Clairvaux.

1. Induced Conrad III of Germany and Louis VII of France to take up cross.
2. This movement almost a complete failure.
   (a) Most of Germans slaughtered by Turks near Dorylæum; French nearly annihilated at Laodicea.
   (b) Both kings, with remnants of forces, joined in unsuccessful siege of Damascus; then returned home.

c. Continued Moslem political revival.

1. Nureddin (1146-1174), son of Zenghi, continued process of unifying Mesopotamia; Caliph of Bagdad made him Sultan.
2. In 1171 Nureddin intervened successfully in Egypt and destroyed the Fatimite Caliphate of Cairo.
   His chief lieutenant in this was young Kurdish chieftain, Saladin.
3. Saladin succeeded Nureddin as Sultan, master of Egypt and Mesopotamia.
   (a) Man of noble, chivalric character and great ability; bent on ousting Christian rule in Syria.

(b) Saladin drove the Latin Christians to the coastal towns; reconquered Jerusalem, 1187.

(c) Tyre the only important position still held by crusaders after 1187.

d. **Fall of Jerusalem shocked the west and occasioned the Third Crusade.**

1. Three leading monarchs of west took up the cross: Emperor Frederick I, Richard the Lion-Hearted of England, and Philip II (Augustus) of France.

2. Only fragment of Frederick's army reached Holy Lands; Emperor drowned in Cilicia, 1190.

3. Richard stopped to interfere in politics of Sicily and to conquer Cyprus, arriving in Syria as Christians were attempting recovery of Acre.

4. Philip and Richard aided capture of Acre (1191) and later the retaking of Jaffa and Cæsarea; but there was deep feud between them, and Philip soon returned to west.

5. Richard remained to perform many individual deeds of chivalric valor, but failed to take Jerusalem.

6. Accomplishments of Third Crusade were slight, but Latins in Syria were aided by Moslem discord which followed death of Saladin.

VIII. FOURTH CRUSADE AND CAPTURE OF CONSTANTINOPLE

a. Innocent III (1198-1216) urged Europe to new effort for recovery of Jerusalem.

b. Crusade launched early in thirteenth century to strike first at Moslem power in Egypt.

1. Diverted to Constantinople through influence of merchants of Venice (who did not wish their rich Egyptian trade to be interfered with and who had a feud with Byzantine Empire).

c. The feud between Venice and Constantinople.

1. Constantinople seeking to oust Venetian merchants from their privileged trading position granted by Emperor Alexius Comnenus (1082).

   Venetians had abused their privileges and dabbled in Byzantine politics; hated as foreigners and Latin Christians.

d. The crusaders at Venice and Zara in 1202.

1. Gathered at Venice, there to be transported to Egypt, but lacked adequate funds.

2. Induced to attack Zara, Dalmatian city hostile to Venice, in part payment for Venetian transport service to Egypt.

3. Then set sail from Zara, ostensibly for Egypt, but actually to Constantinople.

e. The sack of Constantinople, April, 1204.

1. Ruthless and barbaric plunder of the great city. Occasion for it was that knights had aided restoration of claimant to imperial throne who failed to keep certain promises made to them.

(a) Leaders of enterprise had been disavowed and excommunicated by Pope.

(b) But the west was not greatly scandalized, since there was some satisfaction in downfall of hated schismatics.

f. The Latin Empire of Constantinople.

1. Erected on ruins of Byzantine Empire.

2. Venice took nearly half of Constantinople, plus many ports and islands.

3. Rest parceled out in feudal fashion among numerous knights and lords.

4. Pope established hierarchy of Latin Church.

5. Line of Flemish Emperors reigned on the Bosphorus until 1261, when Greek dynasty was restored.

IX. LAST CRUSADES AND END OF LATIN RULE IN SYRIA

a. The Children's Crusade, 1212.

Pathetically impractical movement of children; Pope and Italian bishops sent many of them back home; unscrupulous Italian merchants sold many into slavery in Tunis and Egypt.

b. In 1218 expedition of French knights attacked in Egypt without significant accomplishment.

c. The crusade of Frederick II, Emperor, 1215-1250.

Almost purely political expedition in 1229; Frederick at odds with Pope and went out to east while under excommunication; his army partly made up of Moslems; succeeded in making treaty with Sultan restoring Bethlehem and Jerusalem to Christians; had himself crowned King of Jerusalem; Papacy entirely disavowed this expedition.

d. The crusades of St. Louis IX of France.

1. Turks took Jerusalem again in 1244 and followed this with capture of other Christian positions.
2. King Louis of France spent years from 1247-1254 campaigning in Egypt and Syria.
3. Took up cross again in 1270, this time directing blow at Mohammedan Tunis.
   (a) His brother Charles of Anjou, now King of Sicily, sought to keep him out of eastern Mediterranean.
   (b) At Tunis Louis died, the last of the great crusading heroes.

e. Extinction of Latin rule in Syria.
   1. Hold of Latins protracted by Mongol invasion of western Asia (Mongols were non-Moslems).
   2. But in the 1260's and ff. a series of Egyptian successes against Mongols resulted in ruin of crusader rule in Syria.
   3. Acre fell in 1291 and the last remnant of Latin rule was destroyed.

f. Gradual decline of crusading zeal in thirteenth century.
   1. Other interests absorbing attention of Europe: commerce, industry, secular politics.
   2. Popes diverted by new quarrels with imperial power and with rising national kings.
   3. Formidable heresy movements, against which crusades are launched.

X. MORE IMPORTANT GENERAL RESULTS OF THE CRUSADES
   a. Rude culture of west enriched by closer contact and established relations with east.
   b. Intellectual results.
      1. Mental horizon of Europe advanced.
      2. Increased knowledge of Moslem and Greek science and philosophy.
      3. Great events stimulated literary expression.
   c. Chivalric Culture.
      1. Crusades contributed to rise of knightly ideal of gallant, heroic, polite warrior.
      2. Chivalry rose to greatest height in this age.
   d. Stimulus to national consciousness.
      1. Crusades brought together large masses of men speak-

ing common language or related dialects; **and threw
them into contact** with others of different culture and
language. Thus men were made more aware of differences of nationality.

2. Also established common memories and great traditions
for nourishing growth of nationality.

e. <u>Economic effects.</u>

1. Enormous expansion of commerce between western
Europe and Asia.

2. Importation of eastern industries into Europe.

3. Rise of banking and credit system in Europe; beginnings of capitalistic economy.

f. <u>Feudalism partly undermined.</u>

1. Many feudal warriors killed; others greatly impoverished by debt; monarchical powers took advantage of
this to crush political independence of feudality.

2. Stimulus to commerce and industry promoted growth
of town life and middle class, hostile to feudality.

g. <u>Weakening of manorial serfdom.</u>

1. Because of growth of money economy and breakdown
of manorial isolation.

2. Landlord class, putting heavier burden on peasantry, in
order to keep abreast with rising standard of living,
aroused discontent and promoted flight of serfs to
growing towns.

h. <u>Crusades and heresy.</u>
Contacts with eastern thought brought many heretical ideas into western Europe. This was an age alive
with heresy.

i. <u>Crusades and the great discoveries.</u>

1. Increased geographical, nautical, cartographical knowledge; improved navigation and shipbuilding.

2. Aroused curiosity about the east and initiated desire for
direct trade with Orient, which led to great discoveries
of fifteenth and sixteenth centuries.

4. Note thirteenth century Franciscan missionary efforts
in remote parts of Asia, and the famous travels of Marco
Polo.

j. <u>Crusades and the Papacy.</u>

1. Enabled Popes to strengthen their political and religious
leadership of Christendom.

2. But defeated their aims for restoration of eastern Christianity to communion with Rome; they left a heritage of bitterness and distrust which made the schism more irreparable.

CHAPTER XIV

THE REVIVAL OF URBAN LIFE

I. DISAPPEARANCE OF ANCIENT TOWN LIFE
   a. Early middle ages saw wholesale wiping out of urban life in western Christendom, save partial survival in Italy and Mediterranean coast of France and Spain. These dealt severe blows by rise of Moslem domination of Mediterranean.
   b. By ninth century towns and cities were almost non-existent save in Moslem and Byzantine worlds.
   c. Where ancient communities did not disappear entirely, Roman municipal institutions gave way to rule of bishops and feudal lords.
   d. In the local self-sufficiency of the manorial economy an occasional market or fair sufficed for the business life of a large area.

II. REVIVAL OF COMMERCE BEGAN SLOWLY IN TENTH, ELEVENTH, AND TWELFTH CENTURIES
   a. Norman and Italian attack upon Moslem pirates stimulated Mediterranean commerce.
   b. Greater security for economic pursuits gained by German stopping of Slav and Hungarian attacks; also by Truce of God.
   c. Opening of Varangian trade route across Russia.
   d. Most important were the Crusades.
   e. Fairs and markets multiplied all over Europe; hundreds of towns emerged, not only because of commerce but because new industries sprang up and old ones grew in size.

III. REVIVAL OF ITALIAN CITIES
   a. Municipal life had never entirely disappeared in Italy, and there in medieval times it first was restored.

b. Chiefly noticeable in Lombardy.

1. East-west trade route in northern Europe through Alpine passes to Lombardy and thence by water to the east.
Lombard merchants became leading European middlemen in Mediterranean commerce; Venetian and Genoese shipping men became the principal carriers.

2. Enormous growth of Italian cities in twelfth and thirteenth centuries; emergence to great importance of Venice, Genoa, Milan, Florence.

c. Municipal independence in Italy.

1. Rise of "consular" government, municipal autonomy, destructive of episcopal and feudal rule, in eleventh century.

2. By 1200 the city-state was dominant over feudal powers throughout northern Italy.

d. Bitter rivalry in cities constantly struggling amongst themselves.

1. But even this did not prevent steady growth of rich commercial prosperity.

2. Most famous feud was that of Genoa and Venice.

IV. EMERGENCE AND GROWTH OF TOWNS NORTH OF ALPS

a. Many had beginnings in servile communities which gathered about castles and monasteries; some were on sites of earlier Roman municipalities, but most grew up where safety in anarchic age could be secured.

1. In such communities primitive industries were stimulated and a merchant class evolved.

2. Merchants got special privileges from lord enabling them to extend activities in return for sharing profits, which led to exemption from ordinary obligations of serfdom. Merchants also formed organization for common interests—the merchant gild, one of the institutional origins of corporate town life.

3. In time lord permitted merchants to build a walled enclosure, a *burg*, to protect their community, and this became nucleus of a town. Limited rights given dwellers in *burg* mark beginnings of chartered town liberties.

4. Such primitive communities grew into towns in the period of revived commerce; their earliest history is

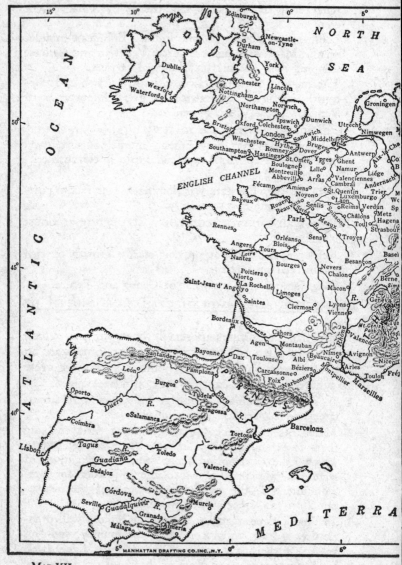

MAP XII

TOWNS OF
WESTERN EUROPE
IN THE
THIRTEENTH CENTURY

Scale of Miles
0   50   100 150 200

very obscure because townsmen were despised in feudal society and little notice was taken of them.

b. <u>First great cluster of towns in northern Europe appeared in Flanders.</u>

1. There the waterways of northern and western Europe converged; a great *entrepôt* for commodities of northern Europe and those that came from Italy; moreover, great textile industry arose there.
2. By 1200 Bruges, Ghent, Lille, Ypres, and other towns had each a population of some 50,000 people. Flanders was the Lombardy of the North.
3. Municipal life widely extended through the Low Countries during the thirteenth century.

c. <u>The communes in France.</u>

1. History of those in south of France closely parallels that of Italian towns.
2. In central France, chiefly along the rivers, arose many privileged towns, i.e., towns that did not attain self-government, but merely freedom from many feudal and manorial restrictions.
3. In the north of France the twelfth century saw wide revolt of communes from feudal rule.
   Townsmen formed corporate organizations and became collective baronies; wrested chartered privileges from overlords and became self-governing communities.

d. <u>Towns and cities in Germany.</u>

1. Rhine valley, one of principal arteries of medieval trade, developed series of important towns.
2. A second notable region of urban development was south Germany, because of trade with Venice.
3. A third group arose in north, from Holland to the Baltic, thriving on commerce of Baltic and eastern Europe. Here arose the Hanseatic League.
4. Great advance of municipal independence in twelfth and thirteenth centuries; Emperors dispensed many favors and privileges to towns; growth of Free Imperial Cities.

e. <u>Municipal life in England.</u>

1. Less striking than on Continent, although London became a relatively important town and some ports, such as Southampton and Bristol, were prominent.
2. England was commercially backward, as compared with Continental countries, down to close of middle ages.

f. Self-government in cities north of Alps.

    1. Feudalism much stronger than in Italy, and had reached full height by time revival of trade began.

    2. Hence feudal obstacles to growth of town independence were greater than in Italy.

V. SOME LEADING CHARACTERISTICS OF MEDIEVAL TOWNS

a. Physical appearance: surrounded by walls, entered by gates and drawbridges; narrow, crooked, mostly unpaved streets; unlighted, insanitary, poorly policed; territorially small in area for numbers of population.

b. Greatest variety in form and kind of government, and measure of privilege and independence.

c. Each developed own customs, statutes and ordinances, legal procedure, thus greatly increasing the bizarre confusion of medieval civil and political life.

d. Intense spirit of local patriotism; jealous devotion to citizenship rights; outsiders regarded as foreigners and could not obtain citizenship rights without great difficulty.

VI. COMMERCIAL AND INDUSTRIAL GILD ORGANIZATIONS

a. Economic life of towns, like that of the manor, was strongly corporative and co-operative in character.

b. Gild organization appears first in mercantile life.

    1. For protection against predatory barons and better treatment in distant markets merchants very early banded themselves together in gilds.

    2. These organizations grew in power, regulated trade in their own towns, and protected members from ruinous competition.

c. Craft gilds somewhat later in developing, but in time largely crowded out the merchant gild.

    1. Their origin obscure, but they were very common by latter twelfth century.

    2. Formation facilitated by men of same occupation gathering together in one quarter of town.

    3. Economic purpose of gild was to regulate competition, prices, and wages; enforce standards of work; secure favors and privileges from authorities.

4. Craft gild included all in a given trade; grades in it were master, journeyman, and apprentice.

5. Large number of different gilds shows high division and specialization in medieval industry.

d. Gilds important in social and political life.

1. Mutual aid and benefit organizations.

2. Had own special feast days, celebrations, and religious observances; every gild had a patron saint.

3. Gilds often had political functions; in free cities they jointly controlled or were the city government.

e. The gild system a near approach to Christian ideal in economic life, although in later middle ages it developed abuses: monopolistic domination and exclusiveness.

VII. SOCIAL AND POLITICAL SIGNIFICANCE IN RISE OF TOWNS

a. In them grew up the middle class, or third estate, a non-feudal society, with a different set of interests from that of feudal aristocracy and manorial serfdom. This class grew steadily in influence and by the close of the middle ages had become dominant over considerable parts of Europe.

b. Towns contributed much to rise of strong monarchical powers capable of suppressing lawless, warring feudality.

c. Broke down the isolation and particularism of the life of the manor; were havens of liberty to discontented serfs.

d. Towns partially dissolved atmosphere of early medieval life by promoting individuality, inventive talents, intellectual activity, and an educated laity in Christendom.

CHAPTER XV

THE CHURCH OF THE TWELFTH AND THIRTEENTH CENTURIES

I. SCOPE OF CHRISTENDOM IN THIS AGE

a. Work of establishing Christian Church throughout

Europe virtually accomplished; Christendom almost synonymous with Europe.

b. Christendom not completely united.

   1. Eastern Christianity broken by schisms and heresies since early middle ages.

   2. Nevertheless, the idea of one universal Church prevailed throughout whole Christian world.

c. Two great types of Christianity in Europe: Latin and Greek, with their fountain-heads at Rome and Constantinople

   1. Each had shared in conversion of central and eastern Europe.

   2. Latin Church had shown far greater expansive vitality than Greek Church.

II. PAPAL CONSTITUTION OF ROMAN CATHOLIC CHURCH

a. Constitution of Church fundamentally the same as at beginning of middle ages; but course of history had shaped its evolution toward authoritarian monarchy.

b. The papal monarchy as the *supreme* spiritual authority.

   1. Unchallenged throughout greater part of Europe.

   2. Popes now spoke of themselves as "Vicars of Christ."

   3. Their government at Rome consisted of elaborate machinery, known as Papal Court, or *Curia.*

      (a) The Consistory (or College of Cardinals) nominated by Pope. A kind of papal privy council.

         (1) Members assigned to various functions, chiefly judicial.

         (2) Elected Popes.

      (b) The Chancery, or secretariat.

      (c) The Camera, or treasury.

   4. Papal government possessed immediate and appellate jurisdiction over every diocese and parish of Church.

      (a) Frequent despatch of legates.

      (b) Elective tradition yielding to papal appointment of bishops.

c. Not even ecumenical councils limited plenitude of papal power.

Twelfth and thirteenth century councils, all held at Lateran Palace in Rome (1123, 1139, 1179, 1215), were guided and controlled by Popes.

III. Spiritual Authority of the Church

a. Derived from the nature of the Church's claim to being a divine society, in possession of the means of salvation. Without sacramental grace from God there was no salvation for Christians, and the sacraments—visible signs of invisible grace—were in the exclusive possession of the Church.

b. The seven sacraments.

1. Baptism: cleansing from original sin and reception into fold of Christ. Took place in infancy.
2. Confirmation: took place during adolescence; a strengthening and confirmation of faith by visitation of Holy Spirit. Administered only by a bishop.
3. Penance: forgiveness or absolution for sins contritely confessed. Fourth Lateran Council, 1215, made auricular confession at least once a year binding upon all.
4. The Eucharist, or Communion: reception of the body and blood of Christ. Fourth Lateran Council dogmatically defined the nature of this sacrament: the real presence of Christ in the bread and wine consecrated upon the altar of the mass through the mystery of transsubstantiation.
5. Extreme Unction: administered to anyone in peril of death; anointment of body with sacramental oil.
6. Marriage: Church maintained matrimony as a sacrament and forbade divorce, although marriages were sometimes invalidated or annulled when it could be shown that they were uncanonically entered into.
7. Ordination: the sacrament through which a man became a priest.

c. The mass the central feature of Christian worship.

1. An elaborate dramatic prayer, and a continuous repetition of Christ's sacrifice.
2. Through participation in this sacrifice Christians availed themselves of the merits of Christ.
3. Without the mass there could be no Eucharistic Communion, and only an ordained priest could say mass.

d. Spiritual authority of Church rested on universal faith that it was the custodian of means of salvation; when ecclesiastical interests and wishes were flouted, the Church was able to strike with its spiritual weapons:

1. Denial of absolution to the unrepentant.
2. Excommunication, which meant the absolute deprivation of all religious privileges.
3. The interdict: used against recalcitrant princes; suspension of masses and all sacraments save baptism, penance, and extreme unction; a kind of appeal to public opinion to rise against a wicked prince and coerce him into submission to Church.

IV. EXTENT OF ECCLESIASTICAL JURISDICTION
   a. Covered almost all departments of life.
   b. Ecclesiastical courts in every diocese of Christendom had wide jurisdiction.
      1. It was claimed that all members of clergy could be tried only in church courts, regardless of offenses committed.
      Clergy included not only those in major orders but also crusaders, pilgrims, lawyers, teachers, students, most civil servants—virtually all professional classes.
      2. Jurisdiction claimed over all cases touching church property (which was enormous), and all cases arising out of marriage and testaments; also all religious crimes.
      3. Penalties inflicted: fines, confiscations, penances, imprisonment, whipping, boycott, excommunication, degradation, deposition.
   c. Law administered in ecclesiastical courts was Canon Law.
      1. Most important body of law in Christendom.
      2. Built upon Bible, writings of Church Fathers, decrees of Popes and Councils, and principles of Roman Law.

V. TEMPORAL POWER OF THE CHURCH
   a. Consisted not only in jurisdiction of its courts.
   b. Many ecclesiastics were also feudal princes.
   Pope held princely sovereignty over much of central Italy.
   c. The Pope as temporal suzerain of Europe.
      1. Idea of the Pope as the overlord of kings and princes of Christendom had gained headway ever since Gregory VII had decreed deposition of Henry IV; in case of some feudal states this actually gained expression in the establishment of lord-vassal relations with Pope.
      2. Temporal overlordship reached its height under Innocent III, 1198-1216.

VI. GOLDEN AGE OF MONASTICISM

a. This period was fruitful in a great increase of monks and formation of many new religious orders.

b. Eleventh century saw beginnings of several more austerely ascetic orders: Calmaldolites and Vallambrosians in Italy, Carthusians and Cistercians in France.

Most famous of these was Cistercian Order (founded at Citeaux in Burgundy, 1098), which gave to twelfth century its greatest churchman, St. Bernard of Clairvaux; Cistercians supplanted Cluny in twelfth century as most influential monastic order in Christendom.

c. Monastic movement among canons.

   1. Canons were secular priests attached to a cathedral or collegiate church constituting chapter or collegiate clergy.

      (a) Some of these had long lived under semi-monastic rules originating with St. Augustine.

      (b) Came to appear more necessary that rules of life be adopted for such clergy as town life grew.

   2. Twelfth century saw strong tendency for canons to adopt monastic habits of life and to form orders living under a rule.

d. The crusading orders, Knights Templars, Hospitallers, Teutonic Knights, were other expressions of Monasticism in this age.

e. The Dominican Friars.

   1. Founded early in thirteenth century by the Spaniard St. Dominic (1170-1221); combating heresy the chief aim.

   2. Monks moved actively in the world instead of retreating entirely into cloister.

   3. Intellectual leaders of Christendom in thirteenth century.

f. The Franciscan Order.

   1. Founded early thirteenth century by St. Francis of Assisi (1182-1226).

   2. Ideals and activities: absolute poverty, loving social service and acts of charity, combating heresy, preaching, missionary activity.

g. The above were the outstanding religious orders arising in this age; in them may be seen a widening of the
monastic ideal to include active work in the world.
Strong movement for semi-religious orders seized
upon the laity in this age, also.

Church took steps in Fourth Lateran Council to stem
growth of orders, lest too great diversity of ideals lead
to heresy.

VII. HERETICAL MOVEMENTS

a. Heresy to be sharply distinguished from schism, in-
fidelism, paganism, Judaism, etc. The heretic is the
Christian who contradicts, rejects, or falsifies church
teachings.

b. Approach to problem of medieval heresy persecution.

1. Men born into a divine society from which secession
was unthinkable.

2. Religion lay at foundation of society; attack upon its
authority was an attack on social order.

3. Heresy regarded as treason; also as deadly contagious
disease, or a fire which, if not extinguished, would
spread.

4. Philosophy of age saw roots of all phenomena in ideas
and hence perceived clearly the consequences in action
of departure from orthodoxy.

c. Causes for rise of heresies.

1. General intellectual and religious ferment stirred up by
conflict of spiritual and temporal powers, by crusades,
by contact with eastern cultures, by growth of town
life.

2. Increased study of dialectics. Here the influence of
Peter Abélard (1079-1142) was very great.

3. Disciplinary acts of papacy to enforce celibacy of priesthood. Popes had forbidden faithful from hearing mass
celebrated by married priests, and from this arose idea
that sacraments administered by clergy living in sin
were not true sacraments: the heresy of the pollution
of the sacraments.

4. Reading of Scriptures by laity in vernacular tongues.
Unschooled laymen became certain they had absolute
truth from direct word of God.

5. Wealth of Church and laxity of discipline excited criticism; preoccupation of higher clergy in temporal affairs

cost them respect and caused them to neglect spiritual affairs; feudal domination of Church largely accounts for this.

d. The major heresies of the age were those of the Waldensians and Albigensians.

1. The Waldensians. Originated with Peter Waldo, of Lyons, who started an evangelical lay preaching movement. Movement received ecclesiastical censure and prohibition, but continued to go on. At length excommunicated. Their offenses were, roughly: they invoked right of private judgment against church authority in theological matters, invaded clerical privilege of hearing confessions and granting absolution, rejected some of the sacraments and held that all were polluted by unworthy hands, attacked belief in purgatory, the cult of the saints, fasts, and abstinences, opposed taking oaths.

2. The Albigensians: a generic name for various heretical streams difficult to separate sharply from Waldensian movement; most conspicuous and offensive was that of the Cathari, a revived Manicheism, which became widespread by 1200, with its center in the south of France. Became very anti-Catholic and bred some serious social perversions.

e. Measures taken to suppress heresy.

1. Church reformation. Innocent III carried through extensive reforms striking at the abuses and laxities which fostered heresy.

2. The founding of the mendicant orders of friars, Dominicans and Franciscans, both of which strove to turn heretics back to Church.

3. The Albigensian crusade. Preached by Innocent III and undertaken by knights of northern France, 1209-1228.

4. Papal Inquisition grew out of the efforts to suppress thirteenth century dissent. Papacy erected circuit tribunals to prosecute heresy.

(a) The mendicant friars supplied the necessary body of devoted and intelligent men for this work. Inquisition manned almost entirely by Dominican monks.

(b) Effectiveness of tribunals made possible by general adoption of secular laws making heresy a capital crime.

VIII. POPULAR RELIGIOUS CULTURE

  a. Almost complete synthesis of popular daily life with religious belief and practice.

    1. Church very practical and close to lives of people, insinuating religious value into all they did.

    2. Every enterprise, political, social, and economic, given a religious significance and a patron saint.

  b. Although language of Church was Latin, preaching was done in vernacular tongues; everywhere Church spoke to people in their own languages and dialects.

  c. Veneration of the saints.

    1. Most popular feature of medieval religious life.

    2. Every town, gild, corporation, enterprise was under protection of some saint, real or fancied; fields studded with their shrines.

    3. Celebration of saints' days the chief occasion for social entertainment and holidays; they were very numerous.

    4. Queen of the saints was Mary, the "Mother of God." Veneration of her one of most characteristic aspects of medieval religion; she represented love, mercy, and ideal womanhood; devotion to her was one of the spiritual forces which gave rise to chivalric ideals.

IX. AGE OF THE GREAT MEDIEVAL CATHEDRALS

  a. The architectural memorials of this age are the first great Gothic cathedrals.

  b. Gothic architecture a medieval creation.

    1. Arose in France in twelfth and thirteenth centuries: then spread wide over western Europe.

    2. Earlier Romanesque style of building contributed importantly to its development; but Gothic was very different in that it got away from low cavernous interiors and sought for height and light.

    3. Structural elements: piers or pillars, pointed arches or vaulting, and buttresses.
    These constituted a framework and in them alone reside all the essential features of the style.

    4. Very characteristic in the Gothic cathedrals was rich sculptural adornment and the colored glass set in the mullioned framework of the great windows.

  c. Expressive qualities of Gothic.
  Lacked the repose of classic architecture; had something of energy and aspiration in its ever-ascending

lines; symbolizes well the religious spirit of the twelfth and thirteenth centuries.

d. Earliest example of the new style to be seen in Abbey of Morienval near Paris, built about 1122; more definitely Gothic is the Abbey of St. Denis, built a little later. Greatest of the Gothic cathedrals of France were those completed in thirteenth century, notably, Notre Dame of Paris, Rheims, Chartres, and Amiens.

CHAPTER XVI

MEDIEVAL INTELLECTUAL CULTURE

I. MEDIEVAL MIND BEFORE THE TWELFTH CENTURY

a. Engrossed in mastering and assimilating:

1. The heritage of ancient thought, as bequeathed by later Roman Empire.

2. Intellectual and emotional content of Catholic Christianity.

b. But only a very limited portion of the intellectual culture of antiquity had been bequeathed to barbarized Europe.

1. Marked intellectual decline in later Roman Empire.

2. Knowledge of classic Greek and Latin (as distinguished from medieval Latin) was rare by early middle ages.

3. Church valued classic thought and knowledge only as aid to practice and elucidation of Christianity.

c. Western Europe inherited Roman system of education modified by Church.

1. With decay of government in fifth century Church took over schools and became sole support of education throughout whole middle ages.
All schools either episcopal or monastic; their single aim was to educate for holy orders.

2. Medieval school curricula go back to sixth century Romans, Martianus Capella and Boethius, who distinguished the seven liberal arts and divided them into the *trivium* and *quadrivium*, the standard school curricula of the middle ages.

(a) *Trivium:* grammar, rhetoric, dialectic (logic).

    (b) *Quadrivium:* arithmetic, geometry, astronomy, music.

    (c) Content of all these subjects was very limited, and they were not pursued for their own ends but rather to serve the ends of Christian theology—the queen of medieval studies.

d. The Carolingian "renaissance."

    1. Charlemagne sought zealously to improve the state of learning, even among the laity.

    (a) Handwriting vastly improved in this age.

    (b) Most of oldest extant classic texts date from this age.

    2. The cathedral schools

    (a) Charles required every cathedral (bishop's) church to establish school for clergy.

    (b) These, although suffering greatly in later troublous times, survived.

e. Ninth and tenth centuries, so-called "dark ages," mark considerable stagnation of education and learning, but European mind exhibited a quickening in the eleventh century, which increased greatly in the twelfth and thirteenth.

II. SCHOLASTICISM

a. This was a philosophical treatment of knowledge and analysis of phenomena with the aim of laying a rational foundation for the Christian faith.

It emerged out of cathedral schools (whence its name) and its development was greatest intellectual achievement of middle ages.

b. Very characteristic and illustrative of the growth of scholastic thought was the great controversy between nominalists and realists.

    1. This revolved about the question of the reality or non-reality of universals, or objective ideas.

    2. Realists contended that phenomena are the manifold forms of *ideal* realities which exist objectively.

    3. Nominalists saw reality only in phenomena; but partway between the extreme views (although also nominalist) was conceptualism, which held that concepts of universals were arrived at by reflecting on particular things, universals being real only as subjective concepts of the mind.

4. Nominalism tended toward materialism; realism was a strong aid to rationalizing Christian theology.

c. First great scholastic philosopher was St. Anselm of Bec and Canterbury (1033-1109); champion of realism.

d. Peter Abélard (1079-1142), teacher at Paris, the greatest champion of the nominalist-conceptualist point of view.

First outstanding medieval advocate of subjecting faith to tests of natural reason.

e. Recovery of additional writings of Aristotle, c. 1200ff.

1. Down to thirteenth century only work of the great encyclopedist of Greek philosophy was his *Logic*.

2. Spanish scholars early in thirteenth century provided Latin translations (from Arabic versions) of his works on natural science and metaphysics.

3. Arose grave ecclesiastical fears that pagan scientist and philosopher might subvert Christian faith.

4. The modern question of science *vs.* religion was now stated.

f. Papacy in 1261 nominated St. Thomas Aquinas (1226-1274) to make authoritative translation of Aristotle and write a commentary.

1. Resulted one of most masterful series of works in all intellectual history; St. Thomas' *Summa Theologica* achieved complete synthesis between Aristotelian thought and Christian faith.

2. He argued that there could be no conflict between revealed and natural truth because both had common origin in God.

3. In St. Thomas, greatest of the realists, medieval thought reached its highest development.

g. The great importance of scholasticism in intellectual and religious history.

1. Hard training of wits, mastery of laws of reason, growth in ability to deal with abstractions.

2. Made possible more intelligible dogmatic statement of Christian faith.

III. RISE OF UNIVERSITIES

a. The modern degree or license-granting corporative

institution of higher learning was born in the middle ages.

b. Forces giving rise to universities.

1. General intellectual ferment of twelfth and thirteenth century.

2. Keen interest in theology and philosophy.

3. Revival of study of Roman law.

4. New knowledge from Arabic and Greek worlds.

5. All the above conspired to burst bonds of the cathedral schools and create the university.

c. Origin of many medieval universities very obscure; they grew gradually from small beginnings.

1. Bologna became a center of legal studies (both canon and civil) about 1150. Students from various parts of Christendom gathered there and formed a student gild, or *universitas* (word used for associations of various kinds), and that marked beginning of University of Bologna.

(a) Teachers also organized and established monopoly of right to teach, examine, and grant teaching licenses (the first academic degrees).

(b) Officially chartered as school of law in 1158.

(c) In organization the university was practically controlled by students, and the Bologna institution served as model for many university constitutions in Italy, Spain, and France.

2. The University of Paris grew out of the Cathedral School of Notre Dame; theology rather than law was its specialty; corporative origins were in association of masters rather than students.

(a) Charter of Philip Augustus, 1200, granting special privileges to masters, marks definite institution of the university.

(b) Four faculties, each with its dean: arts, theology, medicine, law. Collectively these were called the *Studium Generale,* which, rather than *universitas,* is the medieval equivalent of modern word university.

(c) Paris a model for university development in the north as Bologna was in south.

3. Origins of Oxford University very obscure; began as colony shaken off by some disturbance in Paris about 1200. First extant statute of university is 1252.

    4. Thirteenth century witnessed emergence of many other universities, some of which have had continuous life.

      (a) In Italy: Vicenza, Arezzo, Vercelli, Siena.

      (b) In France: Montpelier, Orléans, Angers, Toulouse.

      (c) In Spain: Palencia, Salamanca, Valladolid, Lerida, and Lisbon (Portugal).

d. Cosmopolitan character of universities.

    1. Students of many nationalities found at all of them. Those of common nationality grouped themselves into "nations."

    2. Language of lectures universally Latin; thus an international republic of arts and letters arose out of the variegated nationalities of Christendom.

e. Variation in university faculties, but usual ones were arts, theology, law, medicine. Universities became famed in the measure of their eminence in special fields.

f. Number of students at universities very great in thirteenth century; student one of most familiar figures in literary records of the age.

IV. MEDIEVAL SCIENCE

a. Most of ancient science was lost in the west and also much despised and neglected in Byzantine east.

    1. Christian temper of mind considered science inferior to philosophy and theology.

    2. Interest in science confined to Islamic world in early middle ages. There much of ancient science was preserved, and important advances were made.

b. Arab science gradually penetrated Christian world.

    1. Some meager signs of this before 1000; became plainer in eleventh century. Constantinus Africanus (1015-1087), at court of Robert Giuscard in Salerno, translated Arabic scientific treatises into Latin.

    2. This penetration greatly increased in twelfth and thirteenth centuries, owing to closer contacts with Moslem world.

c. Something of the scientific inquisitive spirit of antiquity had taken hold in western Europe by the thirteenth century.

    1. Most new knowledge was gained by consulting ancient

works, but a few isolated figures had appeared showing a thoroughly modern spirit.

(a) Adelard of Bath (twelfth century) traveled widely, read and translated Arabic science, defended natural science, and showed spirit of independent inquiry.

(b) Albertus Magnus, a Dominican monk at Paris (1193-1280), was a careful and thorough, independent investigator of natural phenomena, completely modern in his attitude toward scientific study and research.

(c) Roger Bacon, 1214-1294, a Franciscan monk who gave himself to reforming methods of scientific thought, insisting that truth could be found only by observation and experiment.

d. Shortcomings of medieval science.
   1. More deductive than experimental.
   2. Too great reliance on ancient writers.
   3. Lacked technique and instruments of precision.
   4. Thirteenth century was very great in systematic ordering of knowledge, but less strong in discovering new knowledge.

V. MEDIEVAL LITERATURE

a. Almost all written in Latin down to eleventh and twelfth centuries.
   1. Fifth and sixth centuries saw such literary figures as Augustine, Boethius, Cassiodorus, and Gregory of Tours, but few others.
   2. Seventh century very sterile of literature.
   3. Carolingian renaissance produced some historical works of importance, such as Bede's history, Einhard's life of Charlemagne, and Paul the Deacon's Lombard history.
   4. Tenth century very sterile.
      Latin dramas of Gandersheim nun, Hroswitha.
   5. Eleventh century produced considerable improved historical writing.

b. Earliest vernacular literature (save the isolated Celtic of Ireland) was Anglo-Saxon.
   1. The poem *Beowulf* may date as early as eighth century although it is extant only in a manuscript of *c*. 1000.
   2. The *Anglo-Saxon Chronicle* (begun in ninth century) is earliest piece of original composition in any medieval popular tongue.

    3. After Norman conquest Anglo-Saxon literature went into decline; little vernacular literature of any importance in England until Langland and Chaucer in fourteenth century.

c. Chief vernacular literature of medieval times was in romance languages, especially French.

    1. *Chansons de geste* of twelfth and thirteenth centuries, written in northern French: poetry of chivalric heroism and valor.

    2. Simultaneously troubadour lyric poetry flourished in south of France—Provence. Also feudal in character, but theme rather is chivalric love.

    3. The courtly epics of thirteenth century France. Less national than *chansons de geste*—more expressive of cosmopolitan feudal society; also exploited romances of antiquity.

    4. Rich production of *fabliaux* (expressive of *bourgeois* life in growing towns); also allegorical poetry, mystery and miracle plays.

    5. French prose literature appears also in this age. Villehardouin's history of Fourth Crusade.

d. Vernacular literature of other countries followed French fashions but was less rich before 1300.

    1. From Spain came *Poema del Cid*.

    2. Germany produced the minnesongs (troubadour influence), some notable hero epics, especially the *Niebelungenlied*, and some courtly epics.

    3. A poetic movement in the vernacular took place in early thirteenth century Italy, St. Francis of Assisi being its chief representative.

e. Greatest of all medieval literature was the work of the Italian, Dante Alighieri, 1265-1321. Medieval literature, religion, and polity find their culminating and highest artistic expression in him. His *Divine Comedy* is perhaps the greatest poem of our civilization.

Chapter XVII

IMPERIAL HISTORY, 1190-1282

I. Reign of the Emperor Henry VI, 1190-1197

a. Son and successor of Frederick Barbarossa.

b. The Sicilian marriage.
   1. In 1186 Henry had married Constance, heiress to Norman Kingdom of Naples and Sicily.
   2. This foreshadowed union of German and Sicilian crowns.

c. In 1190 Henry faced revolts in both north and south.
   1. Feudal revolt in Germany led by Henry the Lion.
   2. Sicilian movement against him led by one Tancred.

d. Henry had crushed both movements by 1194.
   1. But a bitter struggle was necessary to secure his authority in the south.
   2. His power then was very great and he began to assert his authority throughout Italy, as his father had striven to do; planned to head a new crusade, when death struck him down, 1197.

e. Henry VI and the Papacy.
   1. Relations between Pope and Emperor were very strained.
   2. Conquest of southern kingdom (which Pope disapproved) and revival of Frederician policy in Italy were pointing toward bitter struggle when Henry died.

f. Henry VI and Germany.
   1. Center of imperial gravity transferred anew from Germany to Italy.
   2. Feudal Germany began to plunge into the great disorders which were the chief features of its history in the thirteenth century.

II. Disputed Election of 1198 and Pope Innocent III

a. Henry VI's son, Frederick, born of Constance in 1194, was only three years of age; moreover, many German princes wishing to break the development of hereditary succession, chose to set him aside.
   1. One faction supported Philip, Duke of Suabia, a Hohenstaufen and brother of Henry VI.
   2. Another faction, partisans of Guelf family, chose Otto of Brunswick, son of Henry the Lion.

b. Innocent III, almost simultaneously ascended papal throne (1198) and sought to be arbiter of the dispute.

Exploited situation to get from both promises against

the Frederician policy in Italy; at length recognized
Otto.

c. Philip's arms triumphed in Germany and perhaps
only his murder in 1208 prevented decisive Hohenstaufen triumph.

d. Otto then came forward and was crowned Emperor in 1209.

e. Meanwhile Sicilian succession had passed to the child,
Frederick, under papal suzerainty and wardship.

III. FALL OF OTTO IV AND SUCCESSION OF FREDERICK II

a. Otto not only failed to hold Germany in feudal
peace but reverted to the Ghibelline policy in Italy.
Result was papal excommunication and deposition by
German princes, 1211.

b. Princes of Empire now turned to young Frederick
of Naples and Sicily, by this time approaching man-
hood.

   1. Frederick had never seen Germany and was thoroughly
   Italian; young man of genius and many-sided talents;
   called *Stupor Mundi* (wonder of the world).

   2. Innocent III viewed this with misgivings and only con-
   sented on Frederick's promise to divest himself of the
   southern kingdom as soon as he had a male heir.

c. Frederick's victory in the north.

   1. Arrived in Germany in 1212; evaded forces of Otto;
   secured alliance with Philip Augustus of France who
   was then at war with John of England, and this made
   the struggle in the Empire a general European war
   (Otto allying himself with John); decisive battle
   fought at Bouvines, 1214.

   2. Frederick crowned king at Aachen, July 24, 1215.

IV. EARLY YEARS OF REIGN OF FREDERICK II

a. Remained north of Alps until 1220.

   1. Displayed constant activity, traveling from one part of
   Germany to another, holding diets, dispensing justice,
   bestowing charters.

   2. An era of peace and recovery.

   3. Frederick secured assent of princes to election of his
   son Henry as his successor, 1220.

      (a) But the price for this was a recognition of extensive
      political privileges to feudality.

    (b) Frederick's primary ambitions were Italian and imperial.

b. Frederick returned to Italy and received imperial crown in 1220.

1. Exhibited same energy in Sicilian kingdom he had shown in north, but followed different policy.
2. Frederick one of the first modern absolutists in Sicily, crushing feudal independence and centralizing crown authority; laid heavy hand on ecclesiastical affairs.

c. Early troubles with Pope; Frederick's crusade.

1. Frederick in 1215 had, somewhat impulsively, taken a vow to go upon a crusade.
   This gave the Pope a trump card, for he could legitimately inflict religious punishment on Frederick if he failed to execute vow, which Frederick became reluctant to do.
2. Pope Honorius III, 1216-1227, showed great patience with Frederick, neither pressing him to execute his vow nor to abandon the Sicilian Kingdom.
3. But Gregory IX, who came in 1227, virtually forced Frederick to launch his crusade.
   (a) Frederick set sail, then turned back, alleging illness; Pope excommunicated him.
   (b) Frederick set out again, without the ban having been lifted; therefore it was renewed (since no excommunicated person was permitted to be a crusader).
   Pope forbade the military orders in the east to obey him and ordered an interdict wherever Frederick might be.
   (c) The crusade achieved some political success but when Frederick reached home again Gregory was stirring up a crusade against his Italian dominions.
4. Frederick easily successful and made peace with Pope in 1230.

d. Germany during these years.

1. Country governed by Frederick's young son Henry under regency of Archbishop of Cologne.
2. Murder of latter in 1225 began new disorders among feudality.
3. Frederick's policy was to allow feudality larger privileges, thus sacrificing more crown rights in Germany.
   This policy Henry came to disapprove.

V. Reign of Frederick II (Second Part)

a. In Italy the 1230's saw development of bitter civil war, arising out of Frederick's effort to extend his Sicilian absolutism over the Italian peninsula.

1. Aimed at Cæsarian authority over Italian towns.
2. Lombard League revived; Guelf-Ghibelline feud raged.
3. Frederick triumphed at Cortenuova in 1237.

b. Pope Gregory IX sided with Lombard League.

1. Frederick excommunicated again in 1239.
2. Both Pope and Emperor appealed to the public opinion of Europe; Frederick was denounced as a tyrant who sought to enslave the Church; Emperor charged Pope with striving to humble and crush all secular powers.
3. This became the bitterest of all phases of the Pope-Emperor struggle.
4. In 1241 Gregory died, but new Pope, Innocent IV, continued the struggle, withdrawing to Lyons in France, there invoking a Council and hurling anew the papal anathema at Frederick.

c. When Frederick died in 1250 the great struggle against the Papacy and municipal liberty in Italy was still undecided.

1. But very soon afterward the imperial cause was ruined and Guelfic powers triumphed generally, as did the Pope.
2. Latter thirteenth century saw disappearance of central government in Italy.

d. German affairs

1. In 1234 Henry revolted against Frederick, and this led to Emperor's return in 1235.
   (a) Henry crushed and imprisoned for life.
   (b) Frederick enjoyed a short-lived triumph.
2. Frederick secured election of his son, Conrad IV, to reign in Germany.
   He reversed his father's policy of favoring feudality and sought to enfranchise the towns, which led to much conflict; serious repercussions in Germany from the struggle of Frederick with Gregory IX and Innocent IV.
3. Party of princes raised up Henry Raspe of Thuringia as anti-king, 1246-1247.
4. Then Count William of Holland was chosen anti-king.

He kept up struggle against Conrad to latter's death in 1254 and then died himself in 1256.

e. Character of Frederick II.

1. Brilliant intellectual attainments, but very little Christian piety can be discerned in him.
   Product of cosmopolitan culture of Sicily; more interested in secular science than in religion; generally accused of being an unbeliever in Christianity.
2. He sought to revive the prerogatives of the pagan Roman Empire and in so doing to stamp out feudal, municipal, and ecclesiastical liberty.
3. Probably greatest enemy the medieval Church knew.

VI. END OF THE HOHENSTAUFEN

a. Conrad IV of Germany was survived by one son, Conradin.

b. Frederick's son Manfred succeeded in Sicily.

1. Sought to continue father's policy.
2. In 1266 Pope offered Kingdom of Naples and Sicily to Charles of Anjou, brother of King of France.

c. French conquest of southern kingdom; Manfred defeated and slain; Charles of Anjou received kingdom from Pope.

d. Conradin sought to overturn the Anjou régime; was taken and executed at Naples, 1268.

VII. SICILIAN VESPERS, 1282

a. French régime in Sicily failed to conciliate the old Hohenstaufen party.

b. Ambitions of Aragon in Sicily.

1. Rising Spanish Kingdom of Aragon disliked French aggrandizement in Sicily.
2. King Peter III of Aragon married daughter of Manfred.

c. On Easter Tuesday, 1282, general rising throughout Sicily (the famous Vespers) entirely overturned House of Anjou. Aragon took its place.

1. Pope declared Peter deposed, without success.
2. House of Anjou kept Naples and the Italian mainland part of the kingdom.
3. This was opening chapter of Franco-Spanish duel for dominion in the now dismembered Italy.

VIII. GREAT INTERREGNUM IN GERMANY

  a. After death of William of Holland princes sought to elect (1257), but could not agree.

    Divided between Alfonso of Castile and Richard of Cornwall, no German being put forward. Both claimed crown; Alfonso never came to Germany, but Richard made one attempt.

  b. Rudolph of Habsburg, a south German prince of influence and ability, was unanimously chosen, and the Empire was reconstituted, 1273.

    1. But regalian rights were gone and Rudolph had to depend on his own private resources.

    2. He restored feudal peace and revived imperial influence slightly.

    Struck down the rising power of Bohemia and appropriated to his own family the duchies of Austria, Styria, Carinthia, and Carniola, laying the foundation of Habsburg territorial power on the upper Danube. (1278.)

  c. Rudolph abandoned Italy and allowed it to go its way.

    Holy Roman Empire was rather the German Empire from this time forward, although some later Emperors did strive for Italian dominion.

IX. ITALY AND GERMANY AT CLOSE OF THIRTEENTH CENTURY

  a. Centrifugal forces are triumphant over the imperial power.

    1. This is opposite of tendency seen in France, England, and Spanish kingdoms at the same time.

    2. Imperialism less strong than either feudalism, Church, towns, or the political nationalism now rising in western Europe.

  b. Destruction of central government in Italy gave free play to municipal independence and warfare.

    1. Italy seething with party and inter-urban as well as feudal warfare at close of century.

    2. Pope's position was therefore insecure and dangerous.

  c. Condition of Germany differed from that of Italy primarily in that feudal rather than municipal powers were in the ascendant.

THE EXTENSION OF THE
CAPETIAN DOMAIN
IN THE TWELFTH AND
THIRTEENTH CENTURIES

■ Early Capetian Domain

▨ Acquisitions of Philip
Augustus

▨ Acquisitions of Louis IX
and Philip III

▦ Acquisitions of Philip IV

Scale of Miles
0   25   50   75   100

ENGLAND

ENGLISH CHANNEL

Saint-Omer
Brugge FLANDERS Ghent
Arras
Amiens
Rouen
VERMANDOIS
Laon
Reims

KINGDOM
OF
GERMANY

Meuse R.
Moselle R.
Rhine R.

NORMANDY

BRITTANY

MAINE

BLOIS

Paris

CHAMPAGNE

Nantes

Tours

ANJOU

TOURAINE

POITOU

Poitiers

BERRY

Bourges

BURGUNDY

Saône R.

KINGDOM

OF

ARLES

La Rochelle

LA MARCHE

Clermont

AUVERGNE

Lyons

GUIENNE

Bordeaux

Garonne R.

Lot R.

LANGUEDOC

Avignon

Arles

GASCONY

Bayonne

Muret
Toulouse
Montpellier

Béziers
Carcassonne
Narbonne

K. OF
NAVARRE

KINGDOM OF
ARAGON

MEDITERRANEAN
SEA

Rhône R.

MANHATTAN DRAFTING CO. INC., N.Y.

1. Germany disintegrated into petty feudal particularism out of which new feudal powers were slowly to arise.
2. German towns, too, were securing independence through formation of leagues of mutual aid and defence.

d. German political domination in Europe had shrunk greatly with the crippling of the Empire; German influence over Slavic peoples of Central Europe weakening, and the great *Drang nach Osten* (German eastern expansion) slowing down.

Last great feature of *Drang nach Osten* was conquest of Prussia by Order of the Teutonic Knights in middle thirteenth century. This had been started in 1231 and continued until whole Baltic coast up to Gulf of Finland was Christianized and Germanized.

CHAPTER XVIII

FRANCE AND ENGLAND TO c. 1270

I. EARLY CAPETIAN MONARCHY IN FRANCE

a. In 987 Hugh Capet became king of *Francia Occidentalis*, or West Frankish Kingdom.
   1. The last Carolingian, Louis V, 986-87, had been killed accidentally without leaving direct heir.
   2. Hugh chosen by assembly of bishops and nobles.

b. France in early Capetian times.
   1. Variety of racial stocks and cultures: Franks, Normans, Roman provincials, Basques, Celts, Goths, Provençals.
   2. Pronounced difference between north and south, Languedoeil and Languedoc, the Loire river roughly dividing the two; north more Germanic, and south more akin to Italy and Spain.
   3. Kingdom was a mass of nearly independent principalities.
      Principal ones: Flanders, Normandy, Burgundy, Brittany, Blois, Champagne, Anjou, Aquitaine, Gascony, Toulouse.

c. The first four Capetian kings were: Hugh, 987-96; Robert, 996-1031; Henry I, 1031-1060; Philip I, 1060-1108.

    1. These kings did little more than keep monarchy alive and establish hereditary succession.

    2. Relations with Church very close.

    3. Under them the tradition of association between Normans, Bretons, Gascons, Provençals, etc., was nourished.

    4. Their resources consisted entirely of their own hereditary landed possessions: Duchy or Isle de France, lands around Paris and Orléans.

II. ENGLAND AND NORMANDY (TO 1154)

  a. Anglo-Saxon England unified in ninth-tenth centuries by Alfred the Great and his successors of House of Wessex.

    1. But monarchy was not very strong.

    2. Much primitive "democracy" survived in villages, hundreds, and shires.

    3. Tendencies toward feudalism.

    4. Central government consisted of Witanagemot: council of leading men led by king whom it elected.

  b. The Duchy of Normandy in tenth and eleventh centuries.

    1. Founded by Duke Rollo, 911.

    2. Series of able dukes built up strong territorial power; most powerful vassals of French kings; all the while Normandy became French in culture.

    3. Duke William II (the Conqueror), 1035-1087, possessed ability and ambition, plus a piety which won favor of Papacy.

  c. The Norman conquest of England, 1066.

    1. Last Anglo-Saxon king was Edward the Confessor, 1042-1066.

      (a) His mother a Norman; he had lived for twenty-five years in Normandy, before 1042; favored penetration of England by Normans.

      (b) Hence arose Anglo-Saxon national reaction against Norman influence; led by Godwin, earl of Wessex.

    2. When Edward died in 1066 there arose dispute over succession, for he left no direct heirs.

      (a) William of Normandy, a kinsman, claimed crown.

      (b) Witan chose Harold, son of Godwin.

    3. William organized an expedition, offering to Norman followers the promise of English lands.

    Secured support of Pope Alexander II by representing

Harold as an oath-breaker and opponent of Church reform.

4. Battle of Hastings, Oct. 14, 1066, settled the issue.

   (a) Witan submitted to William, who was crowned at Westminster by Archbishop of Canterbury on Christmas Day, 1066.

d. Some important consequences of conquest for England.

1. William established powerful feudal monarchy.

   (a) Kept forty per cent. of land in own hands as private estate, becoming wealthiest proprietor in country.

   (b) Imposed feudal obligations on English barons, bishops and abbots.

   (c) Took control of ecclesiastical affairs and executed Hildebrandine reforms.

2. Norman feudalism and French-speaking feudal aristocracy, lay and ecclesiastical, were established.

   (a) But little violence done to Anglo-Saxon shires and hundreds; much that was Anglo-Saxon in English life lived on.

   Witan became feudal great council (*Magnum Concilium*).

3. For several centuries there were virtually two Englands, Norman and Anglo-Saxon.

e. England and Normandy under the Conqueror's sons.

1. William left England to William Rufus, Normandy to Robert, and a large fortune to Henry.

2. Reign of William Rufus, 1087-1100.

   (a) One of violence and tyranny.

   (b) Quarrel with Robert of Normandy.

3. Henry I as King of England, 1100-1135.

   (a) Quarrel with Robert ended when Henry got Normandy also, 1106.

   (b) His reign in England marks progress toward closing breach between Norman and Anglo-Saxon; married Matilda, princess of former Anglo-Saxon house of Wessex.

   (c) Important constitutional developments in his time were creation of Council of Ministers, a small or privy council within the Great Council, and the institution of itinerant justices or circuit courts.

f. <u>Anarchy in Stephen's reign, 1135-1154</u>.
1. Henry I left no direct heir, but had striven to secure succession to his daughter Matilda.
2. Stephen of Blois, grandson of William the Conqueror through his daughter Adela, claimed throne, and got it. Under him the new monarchy almost fell to pieces.
3. Anarchy made worse by landing in England of Matilda and her husband Geoffrey, Count of Anjou, in effort to gain crown for their son Henry of Anjou.
4. By 1150 young Henry Plantagenet, of Anjou, had gained all Normandy, and in 1153 he forced Stephen to designate him as heir to England.

g. The Angevin "empire," 1154 ff.
1. Henry of Anjou became king of England, 1154.
2. Henry had inherited from his father, Geoffrey, the French counties of Anjou, Maine, and Touraine; and in 1152 he had married Eleanor, heiress of Aquitaine.
3. Thus a great feudal empire embracing England and half of France was gathered together under one head.

III. <u>ENGLAND UNDER HENRY II, 1154-1189</u>
a. One of England's most energetic and most important kings.
b. Restored and developed Henry I's machinery of government which had fallen to ruin under Stephen.
c. Originated English jury system, enlarged jurisdiction of royal courts, developed the common law.
d. Changed military system from simple feudal levy; developed a paid professional body of knights who would go anywhere and fight anybody at any time; for England alone he virtually revived the old Anglo-Saxon *fyrd* (liability to military service of all freeholders).
e. Henry strove to extend control over Church and clergy.
1. Conflict developed between royal and ecclesiastical courts (Council of Clarendon, 1164).
2. Secured nomination of his Chancellor Thomas à Becket to See of Canterbury, 1162, as means of reducing Church to his system.
3. Becket changed from king's man to defender of ecclesiastical liberties; bitter contest ensued.

4. Group of king's knights, without his knowledge, murdered Becket in Canterbury cathedral, 1170.

   (a) Henry seriously compromised; performed penance and strove to placate public opinion.

   (b) Becket canonized and became favorite English saint.

5. Becket's martyrdom enhanced independence of English Church.

f. Last years of Henry's reign marred by other troubles: revolt of barons, 1173, and quarrels with his sons. Died while preparing crusade, 1189.

IV. REVIVING ROYAL POWER IN FRANCE UNDER LOUIS VI AND LOUIS VII

a. There were two principal lines of growth:

1. Increase of royal domain.
2. Increase of royal justice.

b. Louis VI, the Fat, 1108-1137.

1. Consolidated authority in Isle de France by overthrowing small vassals.
2. Gave aid to towns and Church against baronial oppression.
3. Had able minister in Suger, Abbot of St. Denis.
4. Some awakening of national spirit in north of France.
5. Isle de France was chief center of twelfth century renaissance north of Alps.
   This increased its prestige.

c. Early years of reign of Louis VII, 1137-1150.

1. Ambitious and energetic, but less able than father.
2. First eight years fortunate ones, despite serious quarrel with Pope; acquired several fortresses on Norman frontier which Louis VI vainly sought.
3. Participation in Second Crusade (1147-1150) gave setback to crown prestige.

d. The loss of Aquitaine.

1. Louis VII in 1137 had married Eleanor, heiress of great duchy of Aquitaine, which thus passed to Louis. An enormous augmentation of royal power.
2. Estrangement developed between King and Queen and Louis sought annulment of marriage.

      (a) This was secured in 1152.
3. Eleanor then married Henry of Anjou (soon to be king of England), who claimed and got Aquitaine.

e. Louis now greatly overshadowed by his vassal Henry, for English king held as fiefs from French crown more than one-third of all France.

f. Last years of Louis' reign saw Henry II rendered less formidable by his quarrels with Church and barons.

g. Despite some great errors of policy Louis VII's reign showed increase of royal influence.
1. Continued growth of national feeling.
2. Continued crown aid to Church and towns against baronial oppression.
3. Crown had aided lesser lords to free themselves from greater lords and become liegemen of king.

V. PHILIP AUGUSTUS AND THE TRIUMPH OF FRENCH ROYAL POWER, 1180-1223
a. The Flemish war, 1181-1183.
1. Philip married Isabella, daughter of Count of Hainault, securing Artois as dowry.
2. Fears of vassals in north and east aroused; Count of Flanders headed coalition against Philip.
3. Philip won and extorted Vermandois from Flanders.

b. Acquisition of Angevin lands.
1. Philip steadily sought to undermine the position of English kings in France, intriguing against Henry II, Richard (1189-1199), and John (1199-1216).
2. Blunders and misgovernment of John at length played into Philip's hands; in 1204 all fiefs held in France by English king, save Gascony and Poitou, were in Philip's possession.

c. The great coalition against Philip and the Battle of Bouvines, 1214.
1. John did not cease to seek recovery of his lost French fiefs and remained at war with Philip.
2. In 1213, at a time when John was quarreling with Pope Innocent III, Philip planned a crusade against John. This was averted by John's submission to Pope.
3. Count of Flanders had refused to aid Philip and Philip turned upon him.
(a) Count allied himself with John, lord of Lorraine and Holland, and Emperor Otto IV.
(b) Philip attacked from two directions: John led expedition which landed at La Rouchelle, while Otto IV and his allies struck in the north.

(c) John's expedition routed by Philip's son Louis; Philip defeated coalition at Bouvines, July, 1214.

4. Bouvines, a landmark in rise of French monarchy; signalized defeat of feudality and establishment of strong royal authority.

f. French monarchy and Albigensian Crusade, 1209ff.

1. Knights of northern France under lead of Simon de Montfort fell upon Languedoc, principal center of thirteenth century heresy.

Land of independent nobles and towns brought under northern subjection; de Montfort administered conquests in name of Philip Augustus.

2. War continued until submission of Count Raymond VII of Toulouse in 1229.

3. Major political result of crusade was to fasten Capetian authority upon southern France.

g. Philip II's political system.

1. Increased royal domain.

2. Forced feudality to obey crown.

3. Favored clergy, although sought to limit jurisdiction of ecclesiastical courts.

4. Patronized communes and made royal officials of burgesses.

5. Created *baillis*, officials very similar to Henry II's itinerant justices, for government of royal domain; also *seneschals* (in the south), similar officials.

6. Philip worked through his Great Council, or *curia regis*.

VI. FRANCE IN THE AGE OF ST. LOUIS

a. Philip II succeeded by Louis VIII, who reigned only three years, leaving a child king, Louis IX, under regency of Queen, Blanche of Castile.

1. As a result there was feudal reaction.

2. But she overcame all and preserved the monarchy for Louis IX (1226-1270).

b. Character of Louis IX.

1. Rare combination of kingly talents and deep piety; established European reputation for justice.

2. Through him the Capetian tradition of devotion to Christianity was greatly strengthened.

3. Took up cross as crusader in 1244 and never laid it down.

4. Canonized soon after death; enormously increased devotion of French to the monarchy.

   c. Louis IX continued and developed Philip II's system.

     1. Important innovation was creation of royal *enqueteurs* to check acts of *baillis* and *seneschals*.

     2. Established principle that appeal to *Curia Regis* must be allowed from all feudal courts when certain issues were involved: *cas royaux*. A severe blow at political independence of great feudality.

   d. When Louis IX died France was the strongest kingdom in Europe and the king's power was supreme.

     1. Feudal lords reduced to obedience, and church court jurisdiction delimited.

     2. Cities fostered, protected, and loyal to monarchy.

     3. Country becoming unified in spirit of patriotism and nationality.

     4. Roman law superseding feudal law; France becoming a modern state.

VII. THIRTEENTH CENTURY ENGLAND

   a. <u>Reign of Richard I, 1189-1199</u>, chiefly noted for his long absence from England.

   English barons enjoyed large independence, although system of Henry II continued to function.

   b. <u>Reign of John, 1199-1216,</u> fraught with disasters.

     1. Loss of French fiefs, humiliation by Pope Innocent III, defeat by France.

     2. These reverses, together with his criminal tyranny, led to baronial revolt and Magna Charta.

   c. <u>John and Innocent III, 1205-1213</u>.

     1. Quarrel over nomination of Archbishop of Canterbury. John repudiated Stephen Langton, the papal candidate, and seized Canterbury estates.

     2. Innocent laid England under interdict; John exiled clergy and confiscated ecclesiastical property.

     3. By 1212 England rife with rebellion against John.

     4. John yielded in 1213, received Langton, and made England a vassal state to the Papacy.

   d. <u>The Great Charter</u>.

     1. Accumulation of grievances in England against John by 1215; his defeat in 1214 provided opportunity for a kind of national revolution.

     2. At Runnymede, June, 1215, John was forced to define obligations of his vassals and guarantee their rights by written charter.

3. Magna Charta was above all a feudal document laying down principle of limited, contractual monarchy, although it also confirmed freedom of Church and granted some rights to towns and merchants.

3. Charter violated again and again, but remained a program for resisting despotic monarchy.

e. The troubled reign of Henry III, 1216-1272.

1. John died in 1216, leaving a nine-year-old son, Henry, who proved a rather poor king.

2. Henry subservient to Papacy and permitted increase of papal financial exploitation of England.

3. Henry extravagant in support of foreign enterprises.
   (a) Attempted recovery of French fiefs.
   (b) Sought crown of Sicily for his son.
   (c) Aided brother, Richard of Cornwall, in efforts to gain Empire, 1257 ff.

4. Excessive royal patronage of several large groups of foreign favorites.

5. Continuous baronial opposition to Henry.

f. Out of the turmoil of Henry's reign emerged the beginning of the English national Parliament.

1. Leader of baronial party, Simon de Montfort (son of Albigensian crusade leader), in 1258 demanded of Henry the "Provisions of Oxford": reaffirmation of Great Charter, dismissal of foreign favorites, resistance to papal taxation, appointment of permanent committee of Great Council to control crown.

2. Civil war resulted; king defeated and captured; Simon de Montfort became dictator of England.

3. Simon summoned a Great Council, now coming to be called a parliament, which included two knights from each shire and two burgesses for the more important towns, as well as bishops, abbots, and barons, 1265. This was a veritable national assembly, upon which Simon sought to support his régime.

4. Simon overthrown and slain in Battle of Evesham, 1265, by Edward, the King's eldest son, who was the real ruler of the country for the rest of the reign.

5. Edward, who came to throne in 1272 and reigned to 1307, well understood the significance of Simon de Montfort's tactics and policy. He adopted them himself, summoning the "Model Parliament" of 1295.

g. England at the close of the thirteenth century was closing the gap between Anglo-Saxon and Norman-French and becoming a united nation.

Chapter XIX

FRANCE AND ENGLAND IN THE AGE OF THE HUNDRED YEARS WAR

I. <u>France under Philip IV and His Sons, 1285-1328</u>

a. Philip III, the Bold, succeeded St. Louis IX in 1270, and was in turn succeeded by his more famous son, Philip IV, the Fair, 1285-1314.

b. <u>France by this time a modern state:</u>

1. National royal administration, recruited largely from men trained in Roman law.
2. *Conseil du roi,* or Privy Council, displacing in importance the *Curia Regis.*
3. Supreme court, or Parlement, and royal circut justices.
4. Standing army in king's pay superseding feudal levies.

c. <u>Philip IV's subjection of the Church.</u>

1. In line with policy of reducing all France to royal control Philip limited privileges of clergy, encroached upon ecclesiastical court jurisdiction; in 1294 imposed taxes on clergy.
2. Boniface VIII denied legality of Philip's act and threatened excommunication, asserting the highest claims of medieval Papacy to authority over temporal princes.
3. Philip leveled criminal charges against Pope and called for his trial by Church council, sending agents to seize him. Scheme miscarried, but Boniface died in 1303 after severe bullying from French.
4. After brief pontificate of Benedict XI, a Frenchman was elected to Papacy as Clement V. He never went to Rome but packed College of Cardinals with French clergy and settled his residence at Avignon.

d. <u>Philip's attack on Jews, Lombards, and Knights Templars.</u>

1. Expelled Lombard bankers from France and confiscated their property, 1291.

2. Did same to Jews in 1306.
3. Knights Templars, swollen with wealth and no longer fighting crusades, were great privileged order in France.
   (a) Sinister charges of heresy and evil practices in circulation against them.
   (b) Philip, in 1307, seized and prosecuted leaders; under torture some of charges were confessed to be true; Clement V condemned the order.
   (c) "Movable" wealth of Templars went to Philip and lands were given to Hospitallers.

e. <u>Beginnings of French Estates General</u>.
   1. Called into existence during quarrel with Pope.
   2. Philip summoned representatives of towns to meet with Great Council in 1302, 1303, 1308, and 1314; aim was to bring towns closer to crown for taxation purposes and national consolidation.
   3. Succeeding years saw establishment of a national institution, the Estates General, made up of three orders: clergy, nobility, and towns (Third Estate); parallel development to that of English parliament.

f. <u>Last kings of direct Capetian line</u>.
   1. Philip's sons followed him successively on throne: Louis X, 1314-1316; Philip V, 1316-1322; Charles IV, 1322-1328; none left male heir.
   2. Crown passed to collateral Capetian line, the House of Valois, in 1328.

II. ENGLAND UNDER THE FIRST EDWARDS

a. Edward I's reign, 1272-1307, notable for aggressiveness of royal authority and attempted political unification of British Isles.
   1. Conquered and annexed Wales, 1284.
   2. Sought, but without full success, to rule Ireland.
   3. In dispute over Scottish crown succession Edward sought to dictate choice and assert his suzerainty (an old claim), in 1290.
   Scottish national resistance, led by William Wallace and Robert Bruce, defeated Edward's efforts and made Scotland an ally of France.

b. Other notable acts of Edward I's reign.
   1. Restricted accumulation of church property, and levied taxes on clergy in defiance of Pope.
   2. Expelled Jews from England in 1290.
   3. Summoned "Model Parliament" in 1295.

c. **Edward II, 1307-1327, a weak and incompetent king.**
   1. Trouble with barons and parliament.
   2. Defeated by Scots at Bannockburn (1314).
   3. Deposed by parliament and secretly put to death.

d. **Then came Edward III, 1327-1377.**
   Major feature of this reign was great French war.

III. CAUSES OF THE HUNDRED YEARS WAR

a. **Position of English kings in France.**
   1. Still held southwestern corner of France (Aquitaine).
   2. French kings eager to break feudal grip of England which blocked unification of France under crown.
   3. A standing cause for bad blood between the kings. 1294-1303 Edward I and Philip IV had been at war, but without making any important change in situation.

b. **Anglo-French quarrel in Flanders.**
   1. Flemish towns in close commercial relations with England, major source of wool for textile industry.
   2. Towns had standing quarrel with Count of Flanders, their feudal overlord, who leaned for aid upon his suzerain, the King of France.
   3. In 1328 Philip VI invaded Flanders in behalf of Count and established paramount French influence.
   In 1336 Count of Flanders arrested all English merchants in Flanders; in reply Edward III shut off export of wool to Flanders.
   This drew issue sharply: English commercial interests *vs.* French political ascendancy.
   4. Ghent, under leadership of James van Artevelde, freed itself, reopened commercial relations with England and formed anti-French league of Flemish towns, inviting Edward III to assume crown of France.

c. **Edward III's claim to French crown.**
   1. Grandson, through female line, of Philip the Fair; had challenged succession of Philip of Valois, 1328.
      (a) French invoked Salic Law to exclude him.
      (b) Reluctantly did homage to Philip for his French fiefs, 1329.
   2. Now in 1337 he repudiated Philip VI and declared himself king of France.

d. **Sailors' quarrels in Channel and North Sea.**
   1. Long-standing rivalry between English and French sailors in these waters.

    2. Rival kings issued letters of marque and continuous maritime warfare went on.

    3. Sharpened the national feud.

  e. Relations between France and Scotland.

    1. Franco-Scottish alliance, 1295.

    2. England sought to break this league.

    3. When Robert Bruce died (1329), France supported his infant son, David, while England supported Edward Balliol.

  f. Above circumstances converged to renew war in 1337.

IV. TIDE OF ENGLISH SUCCESS, 1337-1360

  a. No serious fighting for several years.

  b. English won naval victory at Sluys, 1340.

  c. Truce arranged through Papal mediation, 1341.

    1. In next few years English ascendancy in Flanders, established by revolt of van Artevelde, was lost.

    2. All the while English and French had continued to oppose each other by supporting opposite sides in a partisan war in Brittany.

  d. The Crécy campaign, 1346-1347.

    1. Edward landed with expedition in Normandy and advanced to lower Seine. Won pitched battle with French at Crecy, August 28, 1346.
Victory due to superior effectiveness of English longbow over French feudal cavalry attacked; yeoman infantry superior to mounted feudal knights.

    2. English marched north and captured Calais, 1347.
This gave English excellent base for attack on France; they held it until 1558.

  e. Followed a truce, prolonged by the Black Death, a plague which swept Europe and demolished perhaps a third of the population in 1348 and 1349.

  f. In 1355 the Prince of Wales, the Black Prince, began campaign in Aquitaine.

    1. Another great French army was overwhelmed by the English (again the long-bow) at Poitiers (1356); this was very disastrous defeat, for King John (1350-1365) and two of his sons were taken prisoner.

    2. In 1357 truce was declared, for France in defeat was falling into collapse.

g. Treaty of Bretigny, 1360.

France ceded Calais and nearly all Aquitaine to Edward in full sovereignty (no ·longer as fiefs of France) ; in return Edward abandoned claim to French crown.

V. CRISIS AND NATIONAL RECOVERY IN FRANCE, 1356-1380

a. Severe defeats unloosed general reaction away from political order developed by French kings; also brought discredit upon nobility for their incompetent defense of country; whole provinces of France devastated and wandering companies of mercenary soldiers from both armies plundered the countryside; 1356 to 1360 France virtually in chaos, and revolutionary movements were precipitated among Third Estate and peasantry.

b. After Poitiers the Dauphin and regent, Charles, son of the captured King John, compelled to summon Estates General.

   1. Estates demanded national reforms to secure its control of finances and direction of government.

   2. Etienne Marcel, provost of Paris merchants and chief burgess of Paris, was leader of this movement, and it was supported by Paris uprising in 1358-1359.

   3. But Charles secured upper hand and prevented any permanent invasion of crown powers.

c. The *Jacquerie*, 1358.

   1. Revolt of peasantry in Champagne.

   2. General reign of terror, ending with brutal suppression of revolt.

d. National recovery under Charles V, the Wise (regent until 1364, then King, 1364-1380).

   Strong king; rebuilt order and authority; cleared land of wandering mercenaries; restored royal finances and built new army; kept Estates General in hand; after disorders of 1356-1360 France glad for a strong ruler.

e. Renewal of war with England.

   1. Charles repudiated Treaty of Bretigny by reassertion of suzerain rights in Aquitaine (1368).

   2. France well prepared and had ablest military leader of age in Bertrand du Guesclin.

3. Allowed English to exhaust themselves overrunning open country and then launched French offensive.

4. By 1374 English held only a few ports of France, and Charles was contemplating invasion of England.

5. Truce by papal mediation in 1375.

VI. FRENCH MISFORTUNES UNDER CHARLES VI; BURGUNDIANS AND ARMAGNACS

a. Charles VI, 1380-1422, only a child at time of succession.

Factional rivalry arose among his uncles for powers of regency; this began the disorders which were to lead France to brink of ruin.

b. When king came of age he was subject to periodic fits of insanity; so that the factional rivalry was not crushed.

1. Party leaders were Louis, Duke of Orléans, brother of king, and John the Fearless, Duke of Burgundy, uncle of king.

2. Party division extended out from court to country.

3. Duke of Orléans murdered by Bergundian retainers in 1407, but his son continued the feud; party led by his father-in-law, Bernard d'Armagnac.

4. 1407 to 1435 this feud raged in France; meanwhile English renewed the war.

VII. ENGLAND UNDER RICHARD II, 1377-1399; THE LANCASTRIAN REVOLUTION

a. Troubled situation at time of Richard II's succession.

1. Last years of Edward III marked by court factionalism, in which John of Gaunt, Duke of Lancaster, was storm center. Strong man and head of baronial party. His rival was his brother, the Black Prince.

2. Widely rumored that if Black Prince died before Edward III Lancaster would seize throne against right of Black Prince's young son, Richard.

3. In 1376 Black Prince died, but not until Lancaster had been checked; when king died Lancaster was badly compromised by connection with Wyclif heresy movement.

4. England in turmoil over defeat in France, financial embarrassment of government, baronial disorders and attempts to enforce old manorial services on peasantry.

b. Peasant revolt of 1381 (Wat Tyler's rebellion).
1. Rising discontent among peasants and artisans since mid-century, due to landlord oppression, the Lollard heresy, and gild monopolies.
2. 1381 insurrection broke out in Kent and Essex led by Wat Tyler and Jack Straw; London joined and for brief time England was at mercy of revolutionaries.
3. Young king boldly captured control of movement and then suppressed it.

c. The Lancastrian revolution.
1. Richard's reign after 1381 an unfortunate one.
2. Failed to feed appetite of baronage for war, by neglecting to prosecute war against France.
3. Great baronial disorder in England; 1397 Richard began strong measures against this and sought to play absolutist rôle; result was baronial revolution, deposition, and enthronement of Henry of Lancaster, son of John of Gaunt.

d. Position of Lancastrian monarchy.
1. Claim to throne not a good one.
Even had Richard died, succession should have passed to Edmund Mortimer, Earl of March, descendant of second son of Edward III.
2. Revolts in Wales and Northumberland; throne very insecure; House of Lancaster needed to perform great exploits to win nation to support.
3. In 1413 a more popular king, Henry V, came to the throne, and he renewed the war with France.

VIII. HENRY V'S RENEWAL OF WAR IN FRANCE, 1415-1420
a. Revived claim to French crown and headed expedition, 1415.
1. Landed at Harfleur, Normandy, and campaigned to Calais, winning great victory at Agincourt.

b. From 1417-1419 he effected conquest of Normandy.
c. The situation in France.
1. From 1413-1418 Armagnacs in control at Paris; but in 1418 Burgundians regained Paris and seized person of king.
2. The Dauphin, Prince Charles, remained with Armagnacs.
3. In face of English peril (Burgundian party had been

in virtual alliance with English, but now were veering
away from them) attempt was made at reconciliation.
Unfortunately, Duke of Burgundy was murdered at the
"peace conference," and the division was made worse.

d. Philip the Good, new Duke of Burgundy, reverted to
English alliance, and result was Treaty of Troyes, 1420.

1. Signed by Henry V and Charles VI:

(a) Dauphin Charles cut off from succession and
Henry V named heir to crown of France.

(b) Henry to marry Charles VI's daughter Catherine.

(c) Meanwhile Henry to hold regency in France.

IX. JOAN OF ARC AND THE EXPULSION OF THE ENGLISH

a. The situation in France, 1420-1429.

1. In 1422 both Henry V and Charles VI died, leaving
crowns of England and France to infant, Henry VI.

2. Duke of Bedford regent of France, governing from
Paris; married sister of Duke of Burgundy to cement
alliance.

3. Dauphin's party carried on a futile opposition.

4. In 1428 English and Burgundians were besieging Orléans, last position north of Loire held by Armagnac
party; hour dark for Dauphin's fortunes, when Joan of
Arc appeared.

b. Joan of Arc to 1429.

1. Born c. 1412 in Domremy, eastern France; simple,
deeply religious peasant girl; grew up in midst of suffer-
ing from French civil wars and English invasions; never
had any political idea save that English ought to go
home and French should be loyal to their king.

2. Heard voices of saints prophesying that English would
be driven out and the Dauphin would be crowned at
Rheims. Voices urged her to go to Dauphin, which
she did (at Chinon, March, 1429). Dauphin decided
to let her try what she would.

c. Joan's triumph, capture, and martyrdom.

1. Joan led successful relief of Orléans, the English ter-
rorized by the "witch"; then aided opening up of way
to Rheims where, in July, 1429, Charles was crowned
King of France.
This fact had a powerful psychological effect upon
France.

2. Resisting an impulse to go home, Joan remained with
the war party for capture of Paris and expulsion of

English; taken prisoner by Burgundians and handed
over to the English, 1430.

    (a) Tried for witchcraft and heresy in Norman eccle-
siastical court, and burned at stake, May 30, 1431,
in Rouen.

    Generation later a papal court cleared her; in 1920
she was canonized.

  3. Importance of Joan greater after death than before:
taught lesson of patriotism; her martyrdom aroused
national spirit and caught imagination of France.

d. <u>Expulsion of English from France.</u>

  1. Last years of Duke of Bedford.

    (a) Henry VI crowned in Notre Dame, 1431, which
offended Parisians, who also disliked large number of
foreigners present.

    (b) Faced rising tide of anti-English feeling, and after
his death in 1435 (which left France in less able
hands) English régime fell away.

  2. Duke of Burgundy in 1435 renounced English alliance
and made league with Charles VII.

  Burgundy now held much of Netherlands and was becoming great continental prince himself; this a fatal
blow to English.

  3. Paris taken in 1436 by forces of Charles VII; next few
years saw fall of English possessions in south; in 1450
they were driven from Normandy; an unsuccessful
English attempt to recover Bordeaux in 1453 was the
last significant military maneuver of the war.

X. FRENCH MONARCHICAL REVIVAL UNDER CHARLES
VII, LOUIS XI, AND CHARLES VIII

  a. After expulsion of English, major problem of French
monarchy was reduction of great feudatory princes.

  1. Princes of royal family in fourteenth century had been
granted great fiefs and they sought their own aggrandizement and ascendancy; so that monarchy had to face
problem of repressing independence of feudality.

  Out of this situation had arisen the Burgundian-Arma-
gnac struggle.

  2. Greatest of these was Duchy of Burgundy, granted in
1362 to Philip, son of King John. He and successors
acquired additional fiefs both from France and the Empire: Franche Comte, Artois, Flanders, Hainault, Bra-
bant, Luxemburg, Limburg, Liege, Namur, Holland,

Zeeland. The last of the line, Charles the Bold, threatened to overshadow all western Europe and be the greatest prince of the age.

3. Other great feudal houses sprung from the royal family were Berry, Orléans, Anjou, Alençon, and Bourbon. Brittany, too, although it had no Capetian house, was a semi-independent feudal principality.

b. Charles VII turned upon these appanage princes; faced a series of coalitions and revolts, but their downfall was rather the work of his successor.

c. Louis IX, 1461-1483, the "universal spider," broke the ducal houses and re-established a strong royal supremacy.

1. Decisive stroke was the fall of Charles the Bold of Burgundy in 1477, brought about by Swiss, German Rhineland princes, and Louis IX.

2. Burgundy partitioned and French fiefs reverted to crown.

d. Charles VIII, 1483-1498, inherited a kingdom in which royal power was thoroughly re-established and with frontiers almost those of modern France.

1. He brought Brittany into closer association with crown by marriage with Anne, heiress of Brittany, 1491.

2. His strong position shown by the fact that he could embark on a great foreign expedition to make good a claim of the House of Anjou (whose rights he had inherited) to crown of Kingdom of Naples (since 1435 under House of Aragon).

e. France at the opening of the sixteenth century.

1. Strong absolutist monarchy; feudality overawed by crown; autocratic king and modern state system.

2. Estates General dwindling into unimportance.

3. Ready to dispute with Spain and the Empire the political leadership of Europe.

XI. WARS OF THE ROSES AND NEW TUDOR MONARCHY IN ENGLAND

a. England under Henry VI, 1422-1461, was very unruly.

1. During his long minority a regency under Duke of Gloucester.

Rivalry of Gloucester and Henry Beaufort plus incom-

petence of King when he reached majority, left wide
initiative open to barons to seek their own ends.

2. Growth of sheep-raising, enclosure of common lands,
was depressing agricultural workers and swelling class
of reckless and desperate men, who hired themselves out
as baronial retainers. Return of soldiers from France
made this situation worse.

b. **York and Somerset.**

1. In 1450's rival party chieftains were Richard, Duke of
York, and Earl of Somerset.

2. In 1453 King's mind gave way and York secured establishment of protectorate with himself in control.

3. Henry recovered and Somerset was restored to power;
York took to arms and Battle of St. Albans, first of
Wars of Roses, was fought; Somerset slain and York set
up new protectorate for brief time.

c. **The Lancastrian and Yorkist factions.**

1. Formerly the partisans of the weak king, the Somerset
element, preëminently the baronial party, supporters of
Lancastrian monarchy which had come to power in
1399. Latter remembered deposition of Richard II,
stood for strong monarchy to curb baronial lawlessness
and defend middle-class interests.

d. **Peace between factions 1456-1459**, but struggle then
renewed; Yorkists triumphed, captured king, and
Duke of York advanced claim to crown before Parliament.

1. Lords decided Henry should conclude reign and then
Richard should succeed, thus excluding Henry VI's son
Edward, Prince of Wales.

2. Queen Margaret rejected plan, withdrew to north, raised
Lancastrian lords and won Battle of Wakefield in which
York lost his life. Followed brief Lancastrian ascend-
ancy.

3. But York's son, Edward, Earl of March, in 1461 captured London and was crowned at Westminster.

e. **The Reign of Edward IV**, 1461-1470, 1471-1483.

1. Parliament declared Lancastrian kings usurpers and
Queen Margaret, Henry VI, her son, and supporters
traitors.

2. Edward showed himself very friendly to Commons,
signifying a new era in which middle-class interests
would be cared for.

3. Fresh efforts of Lancastrians only resulted in capture and imprisonment of Henry VI, 1465.

4. But Edward's régime was weakened by his falling out with Earl of Warwick, and by his marriage with a commoner.

5. Warwick intrigued with Lancastrians (1470) and set up Henry VI on throne again; but Edward recovered throne. Battle of Tewkesbury. Henry VI's son fell, and Henry himself was probably murdered (1471).

6. After 1471 Edward's position very strong; no descendant of Henry VI alive; only possible Lancastrian rival was Henry Tudor, Earl of Richmond, descendant of John of Gaunt through female line. Edward finished out his reign to death in 1483.

f. New king, Edward V, only 12 years old; Richard, Duke of Gloucester, his uncle, was regent and guardian—an able and bold but utterly unprincipled man.

1. He usurped crown himself, 1483, and an obsequious Parliament accepted him as Richard III.
Edward V and his younger brother Richard secretly murdered in Tower of London.

2. Richard a despot, hated by baronial elements, and failed to hold the country.

g. Earl of Richmond, crossing from Brittany, opened revolt in 1485.

1. Richard slain on Bosworth Field.

2. Henry Tudor became King of England, 1485-1509.

h. Henry VII united factions with considerable success.

1. England tired of conflict and welcomed king who could and would govern with a strong hand.

2. Although a Lancastrian, Henry VII governed like a Yorkist, showing favor to middle class and crushing baronial lawlessness.
Instituted Court of Star Chamber (1497) to deal with refractory peers.

3. England entered the sixteenth century with a strong, absolutist monarchy.

CHAPTER XX

THE DECLINE OF THE PAPACY
1300-1500

I. PAPACY AT AVIGNON

   a. Papacy had humiliated Empire, but when it clashed with modern national state it suffered defeat.

   Fourteenth century opened with spectacular humiliation of Pope Boniface VIII by King of France.

   b. Bertrand de Goth, a Frenchman, was consecrated Pope at Lyons in 1305; chose residence at Avignon, which, in 1348, became papal property.

   So began the long foreign residence (Babylonian Captivity) of Popes, 1305-1378.

   c. Avignon Papacy scandalized Christendom.

      1. Most Christians felt Rome was only rightful place for Pope to live.

      2. Rome and Italy suffered from absence of Papal court and loss of dominant positions in Church.

      3. Germans had bitter quarrels with Avignon Popes.

      4. English regarded Papacy as favoring their French foes.

      5. Popes built new capital, which necessitated larger financial levies upon Christendom. Now began the excessive financial exploitation of Christendom by Papacy. Papacy laid open to charges of luxury, avarice, corruption.

   d. Avignon Papacy affected by the widespread worldliness coming over Christendom since diminution of exalted religiosity of age of crusades.

   Yet this was an age in which laity were reading Scriptures increasingly and contrasting the poverty of the Apostolic Church with the princely wealth of the higher clergy.

II. ATTACKS ON FOURTEENTH CENTURY PAPACY

   a. Long quarrel between John XXII and Emperor Louis IV.

      1. Arose out of disputed imperial election in 1314 and papal attempt to force Louis IV (1314-1347) to plead his claims before Pope.

      Featured by renewed attempt of Emperor on Italy, by association of Emperor with heretical Spiritual Franciscans, by wordy war of papal and imperial claims.

      2. Although Louis was neither a popular nor successful

Emperor he got united national support in Germany against papal pretensions.

Imperial Diet (by *Law of Licet Juris*) repudiated papal right to confer imperial dignity, 1338.

3. This quarrel stimulated much writing in criticism of Papacy throughout Christendom.

b. <u>Marsilius of Padua and William of Occam</u>.

1. Marsilius, court physician of Louis IV and former rector of University of Paris, wrote the most famous piece of literature illustrating the rising attack upon the Papacy: the *Defensor Pacis* (1324).

   (a) Advocated right of the state against a papal power grown too great for peace of the world.

   (b) Learned in Roman law, he laid down principle of popular sovereignty invested in a prince who thus exercises supreme authority; hence Church is subject to state.

   (c) Also attacked ecclesiastical absolutism of Papacy and declared supreme spiritual authority resided in whole Church—clergy and laity.

   (d) Despite papal condemnation work got wide hearing, being translated into several vernacular tongues.

2. Another significant thinker was the Franciscan William of Occam, an Englishman who lectured at Paris and contemporary of Marsilius.

   Distinguishing between temporal and spiritual authorities he held first had control over all secular things and denied Church any coercive authority.

3. These two did much to bring forward the theory of the inalienable, undivided, imprescriptible authority of state (absolute sovereignty) to displace the medieval conception of a sovereign Church acting as a guiding authority over the state.

c. <u>Widespread popular criticism and attack on Papacy and higher clergy</u>.

1. Very important in this were the Spiritual Franciscans, a group within the Franciscan Order who insisted upon absolute fidelity to St. Francis' example of apostolic poverty.

   (a) Views of some very radical: that Church should have no property at all, that Council is superior to Pope in authority, that clergy should be subject to secular powers.

d. The Wyclifite movement in England.

    1. England grew very anti-papal during Avignon residence and war with France.

      Suppression of feudal dues to Pope in 1337; 1351 first Statute of Provisors, curtailing papal appointment to vacancies in English Church; 1353 Statute of Præmunire, to stop appeals from England to papal court.

    2. In 1370's John Wyclif, Oxford teacher, wrote vigorously in defense of national government against Papacy; denied supreme temporal power of Pope; went on to deny right of Church to secular power; questioned right of clergy to own property; attacked many abuses in Church discipline; eventually rejected certain doctrines, setting up the Bible as the sole rule of faith.

      (a) Wyclifite heresy spread wide, and thrived upon national feeling against Papacy; Wyclif long protected by court party, but finally forced to leave Oxford.

      (b) The heresy, called Lollardry, was driven to cover by early fifteenth century through combined action of Church and state.

III. Rome and Rienzi; Return of Pope to Italy

    a. Great desire in Rome for return of Pope, especially among lower classes dependent upon his charity; city threatened with ruin in absence of Curia.

      1. Cola di Rienzi, son of humble classes, enthusiastic admirer of ancient Rome, bitter enemy of rapacious Roman nobility, took part in embassy of Romans to Avignon to urge Clement VI to come back (1342).

      Pope refused but promised to return when conditions (very disorderly) there would permit it.

      2. Rienzi led Roman democracy to revolution; set up republic under himself as Tribune; summarily ordered Pope to return; quarreled with Pope, was put under ban and overthrown.

      Rienzi had many ideas in common with the Spiritual Franciscans and others who attacked worldly power of Church.

      3. Rienzi then sought to induce Emperor Charles IV to seek reëstablishment of imperial authority and destruction of temporal power of Church.   But he was sent to Avignon and there imprisoned.

      4. Released in 1354 and sent to Rome as papal agent to

raise the democracy and crush papal enemies in Roman Italy.   Welcomed by Romans and reinstalled in power, but soon assassinated.

b. Policy of inciting citizenry against nobles continued with some success by Papacy, to such an extent that in 1368 Pope Urban V went to Rome.
Found it poor residence and returned to Avignon in 1370.

c. St. Catherine of Siena, zealous for moral and religious reform in Italy, stirred passionate movement for return of Pope, and went to Avignon herself to plead with Gregory XI.
He returned to Rome and died there in 1378.

IV. GREAT WESTERN SCHISM, 1378-1417

a. Papal election of 1378.
Roman populace demanded election of Italian, and Cardinals chose a Neapolitan, Urban VI, a stern reformer who soon angered Cardinals.

b. French Cardinals quit Rome, declared Urban's election invalid, and elected Robert of Geneva as Clement VII.
1. He settled in Avignon and thus began the long forty-year schism.

c. Each Pope claimed allegiance of Christendom and was surrounded by his own Cardinals; when each died Cardinals chose successors.
1. Europe divided in allegiance.
2. Only ways to end schism were for one to resign, or both to resign simultaneously, or for Church to act through a Council.
3. Conciliar theory of Church government inevitably came to the fore.

d. Injurious effects of schism on Church and Papacy.
1. In bidding for support each Pope made many concessions to secular powers in matters of Church government.
2. The two papal courts increased burden of papal taxation.
3. Many bitter struggles (very unedifying) between nominees to church offices named by rival popes.
4. Coming after the long and unpopular Avignon resi-

dence and widespread criticism of Papacy by its oppo-
nents, it was a most unfortunate episode in papal history.

V. CLOSE OF SCHISM AND CONCILIAR MOVEMENT

a. Cardinals from both courts reached understanding
and summoned Church Council at Pisa, 1409.

1. Popes ordered to appear and each refused.
2. Council deposed both and Cardinals chose new Pope,
Alexander V.
3. Gregory XII at Rome and Benedict XIII at Avignon
persisted in their claims, each with considerable support.
4. When Alexander V died in 1410 a successor to him was
chosen, John XXIII; triple schism.

b. In this situation came imperial intervention.

1. Emperor Sigismund assembled Council of Constance, a
larger and more representative Council than the one at
Pisa.
2. Council deposed and imprisoned John XXIII, detached
supporters from Benedict XIII, while Gregory XII
resigned voluntarily.
3. An Italian, Odo Colonna, was chosen Pope, Martin V,
in 1417.
4. Schism thus ended, although last of anti-popes kept up
feeble opposition for several years.

c. Council of Constance sought to deal with two other
great problems: The Hussite heresy (see below, VI)
and Church reform.

1. Council voted in "nations," or national groups (a new
and significant sign of nationalism in Christendom).
2. Each "nation" presented a list of reforms which it
wished carried out.
   (a) Burden of these was condemnation of papal taxation and interference in the various "national"
   churches.
   (b) A powerful sentiment for sweeping Church
   reform, especially of Papacy.
3. Also there was strong element who wished to make the
Council the instrument of reform and hold periodic
Councils as check on Papacy.
4. Pope Martin V, fearing invasion of papal prerogative,
succeeded in dissolving Council in 1418 without reform
being accomplished and without his powers being cur-
tailed.

d. Council of Basel, 1431-1449.

    1. Large gathering which dealt with important affairs.

    2. Fell to quarreling with Pope Eugene IV; he declared it dissolved, and it replied by electing an anti-pope, thus renewing the schism.

    3. Papacy gradually deprived it of support by detaching secular authorities from it; it came to an end in 1449 completely defeated.

e. No more Councils called until that at Trent in sixteenth century.

Demands by reform party for a Council continued but Popes turned deaf ear on them.

f. Conciliar movement failed for following reasons:

    1. Rose to meet an emergency and having done so there was a strong feeling that it had lost its usefulness.

    2. Councils discredited by factionalism and national rivalries.

    3. To many the Council was identical with reform and there was little zeal for this among the higher clergy.

    4. Papal policy of coming to agreements with secular rulers over head of Church; concessions to national kings and princes of large measure of control over ecclesiastical appointments. To a considerable extent Pope sold the liberties of the Church for the security of its papal constitution.

g. Failure of the conciliar-reform movement contributed powerfully to the Protestant Revolution.

VI. HUSSITE HERESY

a. Great schism was an age rife with heresies.

    1. Old ones reappeared, especially the Waldensian.

    2. Evangelical movement swept northern and central Europe; this was a type of religious thought which inclined toward heresy by making the Bible the sole source of religious truth and adopting attitude of hostility toward ecclesiastical authority.

b. The situation in Bohemia in early fourteenth century.

    1. Czechs penetrated deeply by evangelical and heretical tendencies.

    2. Danger of trouble increased by rising Slavic opposition to German domination in Bohemia; the Church in Bohemia was largely officered by Germans.

   c. Jerome of Prague brought from England the extensive writings of Wyclif, in 1402.

      1. These were eagerly studied and expounded by Jerome, John Hus, and their associates.

      2. Hus, rector of University of Prague, became the leading spokesman of the heresy, and was idol of his compatriots.

      His doctrines anticipated those of Luther.

      3. Great turmoil in Bohemia; Hus excommunicated in 1411.

   d. Hus and Jerome appeared before Council of Constance to defend their views.

      1. But both were burned at stake.

      2. Bitter conflict precipitated in Bohemia.

   e. Four crusades launched against Hussites, Pope and Emperor joining hands against them (1415-1432).

      But they were unsuccessful; indeed, Hussites in striking back invaded large parts of Germany and Hungary. Found a great leader in John Ziska.

   f. Hussites divided amongst themselves:

      1. Moderates, or Utraquists.

      2. Taborites.

   g. The compromise at Basel, 1436.

      1. Principal business of Council of Basel was to solve Hussite problem.

      2. Agreement reached with Utraquists permitting them certain exceptional privileges in Church, notably communion in both kinds (cup as well as bread for the laity).

   h. Utraquist Church of Bohemia remained permanently established but Taborites (radical evangelicals) were crushed. Latter survived as a persecuted sect—the Moravians, or Bohemian Brotherhood.

VII. POPES OF THE FIFTEENTH CENTURY

   a. Failed to recover the prestige lost during the Avignon residence, schism, and struggle with Councils.

   b. Refused to place themselves at head of reform movement.

   c. Papacy became more than ever preoccupied with Italian politics.

      1. Gave much attention to the establishment (for the first

time) of an effective government, a modern state system, in papal Italy.

2. This caused further loss of spiritual authority.

d. Popes took great interest in Italian Renaissance movement, patronizing literary and artistic works, rebuild-
ing Rome and beautifying it; another source of
scandal.

1. The new century opened with the Borgia family reigning at Rome in the persons of Alexander VI and his
son Cæsar.

CHAPTER XXI

GERMANY AND EASTERN EUROPE TO c. 1500

I. EMPIRE IN LATTER MIDDLE AGES

a. A congeries of semi-independent feudal principalities,
lay and ecclesiastical, amongst which much disorder
obtained.
Its influence as a European power in decline.

b. Position of Emperor.

1. Still first of European princes in rank.

2. Regalian rights almost entirely gone, along with imperial domain; but Emperors were princes with large
hereditary resources and these, together with a few imperial revenues (feudal aids and fees for writs and
charters) and the force of the imperial tradition, gave
them a weighty influence.

3. Imperial monarchy continued to be elective.
This tempted Emperors to use their office for dynastic
rather than imperial ends.

c. The Imperial Electoral College.

1. Took its permanent form during chaos of thirteenth
century, when princes floundered about for some rule
of election which would eliminate armed contests for
office.
Eike von Repgow and the Sachsenspiegel influential in
providing this.

2. Right to choose Emperor restricted to small body of
seven princes.

> (a) They were: Archbishops of Mainz, Trier and Cologne, King of Bohemia, Duke of Saxony, Count Palatine of the Rhine, and Margrave of Brandenburg.
>
> (b) Status, privileges and procedure of these princes fixed in Golden Bull of Charles IV, 1356.

  d. <u>The Imperial Diet or Reichstag</u>.

1. Originated in Carolingian assemblies of royal officials and churchmen (Empire Day).
2. Gradual transformation into a feudal assembly of vassals of the crown.
3. No representation of the cities until late fifteenth century.
4. Very dilatory body, lacking rules and power to enforce decisions, although able to check action of Emperor.

  e. Constitutional reform movement with the aim of strengthening Germany nationally and placing executive power in the hands of a group of leading princes was led by Archbishop Berthold of Mainz in late fifteenth century.

1. Imperial Supreme Court established (1495).
2. Imperial Circles created: regional division of Empire for enforcement of decisions of Supreme Court and suppression of feudal warfare. They were never very effective.

II. TERRITORIALISM AND LEADING PRINCELY HOUSES OF EMPIRE

  a. <u>Fall of Hohenstaufen</u> left Germany without any large, strong, territorial feudal powers.

1. Jumble of petty principalities rather than a few great duchies, as in tenth century.
2. Out of this ruin arose certain feudal states of importance; certain princely houses carried on work of state-making, rounding out control of scattered fiefs, acquiring intervening lands, bringing aristocracy under control.

   This process called *territorialism*.
3. Great territorial powers arose chiefly in northeast, north, central, and southeast Germany.

   West the stronghold of prince-bishops, imperial knights, free cities.

  b. <u>The House of Luxemburg</u>.

1. Dukes of Luxemburg acquired crown of Bohemia in

1310, and held it to 1437.   This included Moravia and Silesia.

2. Also held Brandenburg from 1378 to 1417.

3. Gave four Emperors: Henry VII, 1308-1313; Charles IV, 1347-1378; Wenzel, 1378-1410, and Sigismund, 1410-1437.

4. Fortunes dwindled in fifteenth century when Brandenburg passed to Hohenzollerns and crown of Bohemia was lost.

c. The House of Wittelsbach.

1. Held Duchy of Bavaria in thirteenth century.

2. Two branches of family, other holding Rhenish and Bavarian Palatinates.

3. Very strong upper German power, rival of Habsburgs; continued to hold Bavaria to 1918.

4. Bavarian duke, Louis of Wittelsbach, was chosen Emperor Louis IV, 1314-1347.

d. The House of Wettin.

1. Leading middle Germany power; held Thuringia and old Thuringian marches of upper Elbe; dukes of Saxony, although only a little of their lands were included in the old medieval duchy of Saxony.

2. Saxony divided (1485) into Albertine and Ernestine Saxony, the latter possessing the electoral title.

e. The House of Hohenzollern.

1. Fortunes founded by Counts of Zollern (Suabia) in twelfth century when they became burgraves of Nuremberg.

2. Acquired Brandenburg (1417) and with it the electoral dignity.

3. This house was very important by 1500, although less so than Wettin or Habsburg; its great work lay ahead of it.

f. House of Habsburg.

1. Greatest of German territorial, dynastic powers of this period.

2. Of Suabian origin, the fortunes of the house were founded by Emperor Rudolph I, who acquired the Austrian duchies in 1278; also held scattered possessions in Switzerland and Suabia and Tyrol; aspired to lordship of all upper Germany.

3. Provided five Emperors: Rudolph I, 1273-1291; Albert

     I, 1298-1308; Albert II, 1438-1440; Frederick III, 1440-1493; Maximilian I, 1493-1519.

  4. Habsburgs acquired, after 1477, Franche Comte and the Belgian and Dutch Netherlands through marriage of Maximilian to Mary of Burgundy, daughter of Charles the Bold.

  5. Leading dynastic power in Europe *c.* 1500.

III. RISE OF SWISS INDEPENDENCE

  a. Group of south German forest cantons, Uri, Schweiz, Unterwalden, in 1291 formed defensive league against Habsburgs.

    1. Maintained right to status of rural communes standing in immediate relationship to Emperor.

    2. Standing feud thereafter with Habsburgs, especially sharp when they held imperial office.

  b. Struggle was carried on through fourteenth century and a number of other rural districts and towns joined the league.

    1. Defeated Habsburg forces at Morgarten, 1314; at Sempach, 1386, and at Näfels, 1388.

    2. Struggle increased cohesiveness of league, which at close of century appeared as embryonic state, unique in character, within the Empire.

  c. Swiss rift with Empire.

    1. Maximilian I sought to collect taxes levied by Diet (1495) and Swiss resisted.

    2. Armed struggle ended successfully for Swiss in Peace of Basel (1499); no more efforts made to subject them to imperial taxation or military levies.

    3. Swiss league remained nominally part of Empire until 1648.

IV. HANSEATIC LEAGUE

  a. In the great political disorder of later medieval Germany leagues and alliances (or *hanses*) between cities, for protection and promotion of commerce, were widely entered into.

  b. Great increase of commerce and town prosperity in north Germany, which found expression in the Hanseatic League.

    1. Originated in late thirteenth century alliance between Hamburg and Lübeck.

    2. Other cities joined during fourteenth century; Lübeck

headed league covering Germany from Danzig to Netherlands.

3. League secured extensive trading stations and privileges abroad: Novgorod, Bergen, Bruges, London.

c. League became formidable, semi-political power and long dominated commerce of North Sea and Baltic.

1. Developed a navy and made successful war upon King of Norway and Denmark (1367).

2. Exerted political as well as commercial influence in Russia and Norway.

d. League in decline by late fifteenth century, owing to:

1. Internal dissensions.

2. Loss of fisheries through departure of herring from Baltic.

3. Attacks on their privileges abroad by foreign governments.

4. Growth of German princely territorialism, which restricted the initiative of the cities.

V. TEUTONIC KNIGHTS AND POLES AND LITHUANIANS

a. Continuation of conquest by the great German order of lands along the Baltic in fourteenth century.

1. The Ordensland, or principality of the Teutonic Knights, reached its greatest power; included Pomerelia, Prussia, Courland, Livonia, Esthonia—Baltic coast and large hinterland from Pomerania to Finland.

2. Vigorous commercial civilization sprang up in wake of crusaders; many towns in this region were members of Hanseatic League.

b. Teutonic Knights cut Poland and Lithuania off from the sea; in 1386 latter powers united, with resultant threat to German possession of Baltic coast.

1. Knights were decisively beaten by Poles and Lithuanians in Battle of Tannenberg, 1410.

2. War carried on, 1454-1466, ending in Peace of Thorn. Vistula provinces passed to Poland, and remainder of Ordensland became fief of Poland.

c. At close of middle ages the great state of Teutonic Knights was very shrunken in size and power, and Germanization of Baltic had received severe set-back; while Poland was a rising power.

VI. Bohemia and Hungary at Close of Middle Ages

a. Bohemia fell more completely under Germanic influences in fourteenth century.

   1. In 1310 John of Luxemburg became king and founded a dynasty which lasted to 1437.

   2. Under last Luxemburg king, Sigismund, a Bohemian anti-German reaction flamed out in the Hussite movement, which was partially victorious.

b. The Slavonic nobility in Bohemia won much power in the struggle and elected a Polish prince, Wladislaw I, as king. Then in 1457 they chose a native king, George Podebrad, under whom Bohemia waxed strong.

But Podebrad failed to found a dynasty, and when he died in 1471 another Pole, Wladislaw II, became king, reigning to 1516.

c. Resurgence of Slavic power in Bohemia, as well as in Poland, suggests a corresponding weakness on the part of Germany at close of middle ages.

d. History of Hungary in this period parallels that of Bohemia.

   1. Received a foreign dynasty, from the French house of Anjou, in 1309.

   2. Estates got upper hand in mid-fifteenth century, and chose native king, Mathias Corvinus—one of the great kings of the age.

But weakness set in after his death in 1490 and Hungary was conquered by the Turks a generation later.

VII. Eastern Roman Empire and Ottoman Turks

a. The revived Byzantine Empire.

   1. A Greek dynasty in 1261 replaced the Flemish line at Constantinople established by the Fourth Crusade, largely through aid of Genoese who were struggling to overthrow position of Venice.

   2. But Empire was small and weak; Frankish principalities in Greece remained, and Venice kept hold on her mainland and island possessions.

b. The great Serbian power of early fourteenth century. For a time the Serbs became the chief power in the Balkan peninsula, especially under Stephen Dushan

(Stephen VI, 1331-1355), whose ambition was to reign at Constantinople.

c. <u>Rise of the Ottoman Turks in Asia Minor</u>.

1. House of Ottoman, or Osman, became rulers of Anatolian peninsula, in early fourteenth century.
2. Under Sultan Arkhan (1326-1359) they made their capital at Brusa, across from Constantinople, and conquered parts of Gallipoli.
3. From 1353 onward pursued conquests in Balkan peninsula until by 1400 they were masters of nearly all of it.
4. At this point they were attacked from the east by the Mongol conqueror Tamerlane (1336-1405).

   (a) Sultan Bajazet defeated and captured at Angora in 1402; Mongols temporarily overran all Asia Minor.

   (b) Turks for a time were too weak to resume attacks on European Christendom.

d. <u>The fall of Constantinople, 1453</u>.

1. Assault upon Europe resumed under Murad II, 1421-1451.
2. Bitter fighting in Serbia against Hungarian, Polish, and German crusaders.
3. Mohammed II, 1451-1481, took Constantinople in 1453. So ended the Byzantine Empire.

e. <u>Continued warfare of Turks in Europe</u>.

1. All Greece conquered.
2. Venice made peace in 1479 to save her trading privileges.
3. After death of Mohammed II no further conquests in Europe attempted until sixteenth century.

f. Modern history opened with Moslem power in possession of all southeastern Europe owing to internal struggles within Christendom and decline of crusading spirit.

VIII. MONGOL EMPIRE AND RUSSIA

a. Vast Asiatic Empire arose under Jenghis Khan (died 1226).

b. Violent Mongol onslaughts upon western Asia and Europe.

1. Conquest of Russia begun in 1222; Moscow fell in 1238 and Kiev in 1240; all Russia, as far west as to Novgorod, under Mongol Tartar sway until late fif-

teenth century—the Kingdom of the Golden Horde; left an indelible imprint on Russian civilization.

2. Hungary and Poland also attacked and even Italy threatened in 1241; but all save Russia soon evacuated. At this time, latter thirteenth century, emerged the Roumanian principalities of Moldavia and Wallachia.

c. Similar attacks on Moslem world of western Asia.
Bagdad, Aleppo, Damascus taken, 1258 ff.; most of Mohammedan Asia temporarily conquered.

d. Revolt of Russia from Tartars.

1. Lead taken by Dukes of Moscow whose principality grew steadily during the long Tartar rule.

2. Ivan the Great (1462-1505) led Russia to full emancipation from Mongol rule.

(a) Founder of modern Russian Empire.

(b) Moscow dukes claimed to be heirs to tradition of fallen Byzantine Empire.

Chapter XXII

THE RISE OF SPAIN

I. Eleventh Century Christian States in Spain

a. County of Barcelona and Kingdoms of Navarre and Aragon.
Derived from Charlemagne's Spanish march.

b. Kingdoms of Castile and Leon.

1. These included old Kingdom of Asturias, from which they derived. It was in the Asturias that Christians had been confined after the Moslem conquest of Spain in eighth century.

2. Sometimes united; sometimes divided; convenient to regard them as one under the name of Castile.

c. Spain was created by the expansion of Castile and Aragon through almost perpetual crusading down to middle of thirteenth century.

II. Expansion of Castile and Aragon

a. Spanish Islam in 1031 broke up into local emirates (counties).

1. Notable Christian expansion followed.
Temporarily arrested by Almoravide invasion, 1085,

but that empire was soon struck down by Almohades' invasion.

b. Castile had captured Toledo and whole valley of upper Tagus river by 1150, while Aragon had appropriated Saragossa.

1. County of Barcelona became Aragon dependency in 1137.
2. Expansion of Navarre cut off by Castile and Aragon.
3. County of Portugal, Castilian fief granted to a Burgundian noble in 1095, had reached lower Tagus and become a kingdom in 1140. Lisbon taken, 1147.

c. Another century saw almost complete extinction of Moslem rule in Spain.

1. Aragon moved down Mediterranean coast and took Valencia, 1238.
2. Castile conquered rest of central plateau, taking Seville in 1248 and Cadiz in 1262.
3. This concluded conquest of Moslem Spain until late fifteenth century.

III. CASTILE AND ARAGON IN LATER MIDDLE AGES

a. Much quarreling between the kingdoms, many disputed successions and family quarrels.

b. Aragon became important Mediterranean power through acquisition of Balearic Islands and Sicily (Sicilian Vespers, 1282).

c. Unification of Spain through marriage of Ferdinand of Aragon with Isabella of Castile, 1469, was the most important event.

1. Both were reigning by 1479 when Ferdinand succeeded in Aragon.
2. Kingdoms not merged; merely a dynastic tie.
3. Spain remained a nation of diverse population and cultural elements, and of many kingdoms (all now under one monarchy).

d. War upon wealthy Moslem kingdom of Granada resumed in 1482 and concluded with expulsion of Moors in 1492.

e. Increase of royal power under Ferdinand and Isabella.

1. Vigorous suppression of turbulent nobility, patronage of third estate, acquisition of control over great military

orders which had grown out of the "perpetual crusade."
Crown sought to found an absolutist state system.

2. Almost complete administrative control of ecclesiastical
affairs secured from Pope; Inquisition set up and used to
suppress heresy and secure political uniformity.

3. Reform of Church in Spain, directed by Cardinal
Ximinez in reign of Ferdinand and Isabella, was one of
the roots of the Catholic Reformation of sixteenth century.

f. Patronage of overseas exploration resulting in Co-
lumbus' discovery of America, 1492.

IV. KINGDOM OF PORTUGAL

a. Its importance in later middle ages due chiefly to
lead taken in overseas expansion.

b. Earliest Portuguese expansion beyond Europe a
continuation of the crusading which had created
Portugal.

An expedition, launched in 1415 against Moors across
Straits of Gibraltar, resulted in taking of Ceuta.

c. Prince Henry the Navigator, 1394-1460.

1. Son of King John I; governor of Ceuta and grand
master of crusading Order of Jesus Christ.

2. Conceived design of flanking African Moslems, by
establishing control of Senegal and striking contact with
Christian kingdom of Abyssinia.

3. Directed exploratory enterprises for nearly fifty years,
with resultant occupation and colonization of Canaries,
Azores, Madeira, and Cape Verde Islands. European
slave trade in Africa began at this time.

d. Vasco da Gama opened up all-water route to India,
and began direct trading between western Europe and
Orient (1497-1498).

1. Blow struck at Italian middle-man monopoly of eastern
trade.

2. Portugal overnight ceased to be a minor power and
for next half century was one of the most important
kingdoms in Europe. She was the first European state
to found an overseas empire.

V. BEGINNINGS OF SPANISH ASCENDANCY IN EUROPE

a. Vigorous foreign policy carried on by Ferdinand of
Aragon.

1. Aspired to control of Mediterranean.

2. Sought to check France in Sicily and Kingdom of Naples.
3. Made marriage alliance with Portugal, England, and Habsburgs for purpose of "encircling" France.
4. Carried on successful war against France for possession of Kingdom of Naples, which (with Sicily) gave Spain powerful position in Italy.

b. Patronage of overseas exploration laid foundation of Spain's new world empire gained early in sixteenth century; riches of this enabled her to maintain vigorous continental policy.

c. Reformation of ecclesiastical order (Ximinez reform), zeal for suppression of heresy, and deeply rooted crusading spirit, made Spain the natural leader of Catholic defense against Protestantism and Catholic reformation.

CHAPTER XXIII

THE ITALIAN RENAISSANCE

I. POLITICAL ITALY IN THE AGE OF THE RENAISSANCE

a. Most Italian cities lost their political independence in later middle ages.
1. Rise of petty despots was widespread.
2. Subjection of most cities by a favored few.
3. Very decisive rôle played by *condottieri*, professional hired soldiers.

b. The age of the despots.
1. Fourteenth and fifteenth centuries in Italy so called because country came to be governed largely by group of absolutist princes and bosses.
2. Despots of various origin; achieved power by brutal and unscrupulous methods; much rivalry, conspiracy, assassination, banishment, imprisonment, etc.—an age of great political trickery and violence.

c. The states of Renaissance Italy.
1. Principal despotic powers in north.
(a) Milan the chief of these; ruled by Visconti family to 1450, when came the Sforzas.

(b) Others (less important) were Montferrat, Piedmont, Verona, Padua, Mantua, Ferrara, Urbino, Rimini.

2. The principal republics were Venice, Genoa, and Florence.

(a) Venice remained free of despotic rule, but government was in hands of a small commercial aristocracy. Her naval wars with Genoa, 1350-1355 and 1378-1381, permanently reduced the importance of the Genoese Republic.

(b) Florence a democratic city-state which brought nearly all Tuscany under her sway. Rule of the Medici family was established in 1434, but it was not an open despotism—rather a dictatorship concealed under forms of republic.

3. The Papal States and the Kingdoms of Naples and Sicily covered most of central and southern Italy.

(a) Pope became virtual Italian "despot" in fifteenth century.

(b) Kingdom of Naples passed from House of Anjou to Aragon in 1435, and then to an illegitimate branch of House of Aragon in 1458 (King Ferrante I, 1458-1494).

d. No semblance of political unity in Italy; nationalism non-existent.

1. Italy an international state system with various types of government from small democratic republics to large despotic powers.

2. Each state against every other state; maintenance of relations very difficult; Italians became first masters of modern European statecraft and diplomacy.

A new political science based on force and expediency was developed; described and taught to Europe by Niccolo Machiavelli (1469-1527) in his *Prince*.

3. Although Italy taught politics to Europe she was unable to devise a system that would preserve her own independence from foreign domination.

Latter fifteenth century saw beginning of a series of invasions and struggles between French, Spaniards, and Germans for Italian dominion.

II. MEANING OF THE RENAISSANCE

a. Broad, general meaning: all the great changes in European life and thought from fourteenth to sixteenth centuries—recovery of classic knowledge and spirit, revival of science, growth of national cultures, secularization of thought, individualism, geographic discovery, etc.

b. Narrower sense: intellectual movement originating in Italy—rise of a new appreciation of, interest in, and enthusiasm for the culture of Latin and Greek antiquity.

c. A reaction away from the other-worldliness of the middle ages and their preoccupation with philosophy and theology, in the direction of keen interest and joy in this world.

III. WHY THE RENAISSANCE BEGAN IN ITALY

a. Classic civilization never entirely extinguished there. Italy strewn with remains of antiquity.

b. Early Italian leadership in commerce and industry, which broke down feudal agrarian society and prompted growth of urban life; there arose a wealthy class able to patronize learning, education, and art. Town life released individual liberty, and prosperity made possible luxury.

c. Violent and thrilling life of Italy: communal struggles, party conflicts, inter-urban warfare, rise of despots, etc.,—all this opened doors to careers, made call upon individual talents and ambitions.

IV. PETRARCH AND HUMANISM

a. Francesco Petrarca (Petrarch), 1304-1374.

1. A Florentine, although born at Arezzo; he studied at Bologna and Montpellier; and spent some years at Papal Avignon; then for many years resided at Florence.

2. In mid-fourteenth century he gave great stimulus to growing enthusiasm for revival of classic studies and classic culture; popularized the reading of classic poets, orators, historians, *et al.*

3. Absorbed a feeling for ancient culture in very remarkable fashion; recaptured the classic mood and communicated it to his age through his friends, letters, and poetry.

b. Petrarch founded new intellectual movement called *humanism*.

    1. Word comes from *humanitas,* meaning the highest and most harmonious cultivation of human faculties and powers.

    2. It came to be thought that restoration of classic culture, language, literature, ideas, ideals, etc., was best means for developing in man the true *humanitas.*

    3. Therefore, the *humanists* were those who, touched by the classic spirit, participated in the effort to restore antique culture.

    Developed many-sided activity, ransacking obscure places for ancient literature. There was extensive writing of poetry, histories, critical works (new scholarship born), and popular literature. Considerable imitation of ancients but much original work, for the classic spirit of free inquiry, delight in pleasures of the world and love of nature infected them.

    4. Humanist ideal became desire to know everything and excel in every field: scholarship, poetry, art, and science —to be a *polyhistor,* or universal scholar.

c. Revival of classic Latin an important feature of the Renaissance.

    1. This helped to kill Latin as a living literary language.

    2. Greatest Renaissance literature was in vernacular.

d. The Greek revival.

    1. Ability to read classic Greek did not become widespread until fifteenth century.

    2. Coming of Greeks to Italy in late fourteenth and fifteenth century (as Turks closed in upon Constantinople) gave great stimulus to recovery of knowledge of classic Greek and ancient Greek literature.

    3. Humanist movement rose to full height with the Greek revival.

e. Opposition to humanism.

    1. Viewed coldly by universities, which were great professional schools with established curricula; they resented intrusion of humanist studies.

    2. Theologians and jurists distrusted its criticism and impatience of authority and rules; it had a pagan flavor and was somewhat disrespectful towards ecclesiastics and professors.

V. Renaissance Art in Italy

a. In architecture came a return to Roman and Greek architectural forms and principles: post and beam, colonnade, domes, porticos, etc.

Greatest of Italian architects in this period were Brunelleschi (1377-1446), Alberti (1404-1472), and Bramante (1444-1514).

b. Sculpture and painting show well the Renaissance "return to nature."

1. Sculpture found its inspiration in Roman-Greek art, much of which could be discovered and studied. Faculty of representing natural objects realistically (which middle ages had not possessed) was entirely recovered.

2. The "return to nature" in painting was more difficult, but here too perfection was attained.

3. The three supreme artists of the Italian Renaissance were Leonardo da Vinci (1452-1519), Michelangelo (1474-1564), Rafael (1483-1520).

c. In artistic creation the Italians of the Renaissance rivalled fifth century Athens.

VI. Principal Centers of Renaissance in Italy

a. Florence the central school of letters and art.

1. Here Petrarch made his influence felt most deeply.

2. Florence enjoyed great prosperity which reached its height in mid-fifteenth century.

3. Church Council of Florence, 1438 (for reunion of Greek Church with west) stimulated Greek studies.

4. The Medici family, Cosimo and Lorenzo the Magnificent, dominated fifteenth century Florence, and were perhaps the greatest patrons of the Renaissance movement.

b. By 1500 Rome had become an even more brilliant center of Renaissance humanism and art than Florence.

Papacy was now almost a secular institution; as princes the popes of this period exhibited the fashions of the age and devoted much attention to patronage of the arts; an age of fastidious and polished elegance at papal court.

    c. Infinite variety in Italian Renaissance; each region had its own distinctive schools and movements.

      1. Other notable centers were Venice, Padua, Siena, Milan, Mantua, Ferrara, Urbino, Rimini, Naples.

      2. Beyond Florence it was rather at courts of princes than capitals of republics that letters and art flourished.

VII. RENAISSANCE COMMUNICATED TO EUROPE

    a. By middle of fifteenth century humanism was fast penetrating the rest of Europe.

      1. Thousands of persons went to Italy for the new learning.

      2. Printing by movable type, greatly cheapening the cost of books, was developed in Germany about 1450 and rapidly spread over Europe; this, above everything else, made possible the rapid spread of the new intellectual movement.

    b. But Renaissance was not merely an importation from Italy; it sprang also from native soil of other lands. Had distinctly national characteristics in France, Germany, Netherlands, England, Spain.

    c. Richest flowering of Renaissance beyond Italy came after 1500.

EXAMINATION QUESTIONS
AND ANSWERS

It is the purpose of this section of the outline to present to the student a series of questions that will cover each chapter of the text. The questions are broken down into the three types most regularly used in Medieval History courses: 1) objective questions; 2) identification questions; and 3) essay questions. As the student realizes, most examinations employ a combination of the three types mentioned. However, some instructors prefer one type over another, hence an attempt to cover all groups in this section of the outline.

I. <u>Objective Questions</u>. This type has become quite popular in history examinations. The title objective is used because the answers will be graded objectively, that is, without resort to any subjective judgment on the part of the readers. Breaking the objective questions down they are divided into four categories: 1) true and false; 2) multiple choice; 3) association; and 4) completion.

A. <u>True or False Questions</u>. These questions call for a decision on the part of the student as to the truth or falsity of brief statements. Typical questions of this sort covering the chapters of this outline follow:

1. Ancient culture was profoundly modified by the victorious spread of Christianity. T
2. Greek culture had not blended itself with the various ancient cultures. F
3. The Roman Empire was divided into five centralized governments called prefectures. F
4. Constantine I was the emancipator of Christianity. T
5. Paul of Tarsus was strongly influenced by Hellenistic culture. T
6. The doctrine of life beyond the grave helped the spread of Christianity. T
7. St. Anthony of Thebes initiated the first great monastic movement in the third century. T
8. The Germans brought legal codes with them into the Roman Empire. F

153

9. Alario, leader of the Visigoths, led his people into the Empire in 397. **T**

10. Attila invaded the West in 449. **T**

11. From the reign of Justinian we received the Institutes. **T**

12. Gregory the Great failed to promote monasticism while Pope. **F**

13. The Benedictine Rule was based on three fundamental vows. **T**

14. The Hegira of Mohammed took place in 622. **T**

15. Charles Martel failed to campaign against the Saxons. **F**

16. The Carolingian dynasty got its name from Charles the Great of the Arnulfing House. **T**

17. Charlemagne's system of government proved successful because the national codes of subjected peoples were respected. **T**

18. The supremacy of the Pope is demonstrated by the coronation of Charlemagne. **T**

19. Feudalism rose in the Middle Ages because of disorder and insecurity after the Germanic invasions. **T**

20. The Cluniac reform came about because of the success that the Church was experiencing in the 10th Century. **F**

21. The Investitures of War ended with Henry seeking the Pope's pardon at Canosa. **F**

22. The Crusades were aided by the love of warfare in feudal society. **T**

23. The results of the Crusades are seen in the stimulus to national consciousness. **T**

24. Urban life was not revived easily in Italy because they never had municipal life there. **F**

25. The ecumenical councils of the Church limited the plenitude of papal power. **F**

26. The golden age of monasticism came in the 11th Century. **F**

27. Innocent III failed to make any extensive reforms in the Church. **F**

28. Gothic architecture was a medieval creation. **T**

29. Scholasticism was a philosophical treatment of knowledge whose aim was to lay a rational foundation for the Christian faith. **T**

30. Universities of the Middle Ages lacked a cosmopolitan character. **F**

31. Medieval literature was mostly written in Latin down to the 11th and 12th centuries. **T**

32. Henry VI's marriage aided the union of German and Sicilian crowns. **T**

33. Frederick II was forced to launch a crusade by Gregory IX. **T**

34. The Sicilian Vespers took place in 1272. **F**

35. The first Capetian king of France was Hugh. **T**

36. Henry II of England was one of the most important kings because he developed the common law. **T**

37. The Jacquerie was a revolt of the French peasantry in Paris.**F**

38. Rome and Italy suffered when the Papal Court moved to Avignon. **T**

39. The Great Western Schism was the break in diplomatic relations of France and England. **F**

40. The Hanseatic League gave a great increase to commerce and town prosperity in north Germany. **T**

41. One of the causes of the Hundred Years War was Edward III's claim to the French crown. **T**

B. Multiple Choice Questions. This type of examination gives the student a series of statements, only one of which is correct. He must designate which one. Typical multiple-choice questions follow:

1. Humanism means (1) <u>the highest cultivation of human faculties and powers</u> (2) recovery of classic knowledge and spirit (3) a return to the established curricula of the universities (4) a strong respect for ecclesiastics and professors.

2. The Duchy of Bavaria in the 13th Century was held by the house of (1) Hapsburg (2) Luxemburg (3) <u>Wittelsbach</u> (4) Hohenzollern.

3. The Hussite heresy had for its background the teachings of (1) Jerome of Prague (2) Mani (3) Pelagius (4) <u>Wyclif.</u>

4. Edward I of England (1) conducted the Crecy campaign (2) signed the Treaty of Bretigny (3) <u>summoned</u> "<u>Model Parliament</u>" (4) defeated the Scots at Bannockburn.

5. The last Anglo-Saxon king was (1) <u>Edward the Confessor</u> (2) William of Normandy (3) Henry I (4) William Rufus.

6. Universities came into being because of (1) <u>keen interest in theology and philosophy</u> (2) desire of the king to control thought (3) the Churchs' absolutism (4) the demands of the people.

7. Gothic architecture rose first in (1) Italy (2) Spain (3) <u>France</u> (4) Portugal.

8. Heretical movements had their cause in (1) the rise of national states (2) the influence of eastern rites (3) <u>the Crusades</u> (4) the rise of education.

9. The Crusades resulted in (1) increased power of the Pope (2) the extension of the horizons of the Church (3) the <u>increase in chivalry</u> (4) the strengthening of manorial serfdom.

10. The leader of the first crusade was (1) <u>Count Robert of</u>

Flanders (2) St. Bernard of Clairvaux (3) Frederick II (4) Innocent III.

11. The Concordat of Worms (1) caused the end of the Hundred Years War (2) <u>distinguished</u> <u>between</u> <u>spiritual</u> <u>offices</u> <u>and</u> <u>temporal</u> <u>lands</u> (3) divided Sicily (4) caused the Investitures War.

12. Hildebrand was (1) King of Germany (2) Prince Regent in France (3) <u>Pope</u> (4) leader of the Crusades.

13. The feudal contract was entered into (1) <u>by</u> <u>act</u> <u>of</u> <u>fealty</u> (2) lightly (3) between serf and lord (4) in preparation for war.

14. The historic importance of the Northmen was found in their (1) <u>contributions</u> <u>to</u> <u>feudal</u> <u>society</u> (2) wars with the Saracens (3) travels to the new world (4) aid to the Frankish Empire.

15. The empire of Charlemagne was ruled through (1) <u>military</u> <u>might</u> (2) the Church (3) elected officials (4) old Roman law.

16. Islam affected Christianity by (1) increasing heresy (2) wiping out its influence (3) <u>helping</u> <u>the</u> <u>Papacy</u> <u>establish</u> <u>its</u> <u>supremacy</u> (4) aiding the eastern church.

17. The Corpus Juris Civilis was begun under (1) Justinian (2) <u>Theodosius</u> (3) Heraclius (4) Isaurian.

18. Justinian's religious policy declared for (1) the monophysite heresy (2) the abdication of the Pope (3) the control of the Empire over the Church (4) <u>the</u> <u>orthodoxy</u>.

19. The importance of the Byzantine Empire is seen in the (1) geographic location (2) lack of internal dissention (3) <u>link</u> <u>between</u> <u>antiquity</u> <u>and</u> <u>modern</u> <u>times</u> (4) type of leadership.

20. Richard I of England was best known for (1) <u>his</u> <u>long</u> <u>absence</u> <u>from</u> <u>his</u> <u>homeland</u> (2) liberalism (3) failure to follow the system of government set by Henry II (4) failure to give independence to his nobles.

21. Magna Carta was a (1) document that denied the freedom of the Church (2) recognition of the King's power (3) means of developing despotic monarchy (4) <u>feudal</u> <u>document</u>.

22. Simon de Montfort was (1) leader of the Peasant Party (2) <u>dictator</u> <u>of</u> <u>England</u> (3) strong supporter of Henry III (4) an objector to the "Provisions of Oxford."

23. One of the principal republics of renaissance Italy was (1) Padua (2) Ferrara (3) <u>Genova</u> (4) Verona.

24. Moslem rule in Spain failed because (1) the Turks lost interest in western Europe (2) <u>of</u> <u>the</u> <u>marriage</u> <u>of</u> <u>Ferdinand</u>

and Isabella (3) the Moslem religion lost contact with its
peoples (4) their foreign policy was poor.
25. The Lancastrian Revolution was caused by (1) the Wat
Tyler Rebellion (2) the declaring of war on France (3)
<u>Richard's</u> <u>attempt</u> <u>to</u> <u>play</u> <u>the</u> <u>absolutist</u> <u>role</u> (4) the serfs.

C. <u>Association Questions</u>. This type of question presents the
student with dates, names and events. It is expected that
the student associate or arrange these facts in proper se-
quence. The following illustrate this type of question.
1. One term in Group II and one term in Group III are
closely associated with a term in Group I. Letter the
appropriate terms in Group II and III with the letter (a).
Proceed through the rest of the question in the same way:

GROUP I	GROUP II	GROUP III
a) Nicea	_l_ Avignon	_k_ Champagne
b) Pelagius	_f_ Philip IV	_f_ Clement V
c) Pepin the Short	_g_ Ribbed Vaulting	_h_ Eighth Century
d) Feudalism	_k_ Peasant Revolt	_l_ Clement VI
e) Cluniac Reforms	_d_ Political Organ-	_a_ 325 A.D.
	ization	
f) Knights Templars	_m_ Humanism	_g_ Flying Buttress
g) Gothic Archi-	_j_ Philip II	_d_ Comitatus
tecture		
h) Boewulf	_e_ Berno	_m_ Polyhistor
i) Duke Rollo	_i_ 911	_c_ Frank
k) The Jacquerie	_c_ Mayor of Palace	_e_ Tenth Century
j) Baillis	_a_ Church Council	_b_ British monk
l) Rienzi	_b_ Heresy	_i_ Normandy
m) Petrarch	_h_ Vernacular	_j_ Enqueteurs

2. Place the events listed below in strict chronological order.
Place the proper number in the space at the left.

GROUP I

1	(2)	1. The Besancon Episode
2	(1)	2. St. Augustine
3	(4)	3. The Cathari
4	(3)	4. Henry IV
5	(5)	5. Frederick II

GROUP II

1	(3)	1. Capture of Jerusalem
2	(1)	2. Innocent III
3	(5)	3. Peter the Hermit
4	(2)	4. Capture of Constantinople
5	(4)	5. Zenghi

GROUP III

1	(*3*)	1.	Leo I
2	(*5*)	2.	Mohammed
3	(*1*)	3.	Attila
4	(*2*)	4.	Louis the Pious
5	(*4*)	5.	Clovis

D. Completion Questions. This type of question requires that the student fill in the blank space with the proper date, name, or event that will complete the statement. Below are a few examples of this type of question:

1. The French *Estates Gen'l* was called into being by *Philip*; it was made up of three orders: *clergy*, *nobility*, and *towns*.

2. On Christmas Day, *800* Charlemagne was crowned in Rome. This great leader established the *Medieval Roman Empire* with its *Merovingian* system of *Missi Dominici*

3. In *622* Mohammed carried on his *Hegira* from *Mecca* to Medina, this sets the date for the Mohammedan calendar.

4. The greater increase of commerce in Germany led to the establishment of the *Hanseatic League*. It originated in the late *13th Century* with an alliance between *Hamburg* and *Lübeck*.

5. *Prince Henry the Navigator* conceived the design of flanking the African Moslems by controlling *Senegal* as a result colonized the *Canaries*, *Azores*, and *Madeira* islands.

6. Medieval intellectual culture is seen in the medieval school curricula, which went back to the *Sixth* century Romans, *Martianus Capella* and *Boethius* who distinguished the *seven* liberal arts and divided them into the *trivium* and *quadrivium* the standard school curricula of the Middle Ages.

7. The Papacy in *1261* nominated *St. Thomas Aquino* to make an authoritative translation of *Aristotle* and write a *commentary*.

8. The *Concordat of Worms*, concluded between *Emperor Henry V* and *Pope Calixtus II*, distinguished between spiritual offices and temporal lands.

9. In *987* Hugh Capet became king of the *West Frankish Kingdom*. He was chosen by an assembly of *bishops* and *nobles*.

II. Identification Questions. In this type of question the student is given a list of names or events, and asked to write a brief paragraph on each. As identification questions are used to determine the students working knowledge of the text or of the assigned readings, he should include in his answer facts drawn from those sources. These anwers should be short but meaty.

Examples of this type of question follows:
1. In one short paragraph explain the significance of the following: Frederick II, Dante Alighieri, Albertus Magnus, Peter Abelard, Innocent III, Leif Erikson, Pepin I, King Aistulf, Justinian, Clovis.
2. Write a brief essay on: the rise of the Moravingian·Frankish Kingdom, Feudalism, the temporal power of the Church in the 12th and 13th centuries, the early years of the reign of Frederick II, the rise of the medieval tours, the Hundred Years War.

III. Essay Questions. The use of the essay type question has held the center of the academic stage for many years. This type of question is difficult to answer and hence the student must give adequate time in preparation.

An instructor who gives properly prepared essay questions is testing his students' ability to 1) _understand_ the material of the course, 2) _organize_ that material intelligently, 3) _select_ the most important events for discussion, and 4) demonstrate _factual knowledge_. The student must keep in mind the fact that his grade will depend on all four of the above mentioned points. They should be kept in mind both in preparing for the examination and when writing it.

Understanding the material of a course is a prime requisite. An essay that will cover the highlights of a phase of history cannot be tackled with only superficial knowledge of the material. A student will be unable to truly understand the subject from one source of information. A good answer to an essay question calls for: 1) knowledge gained from lectures, outside readings, the reading of the text and the preparation of written assignments, 2) the arrangement of the material in a logical manner, 3) drawing sensible conclusions from the proper use of the first two points listed. This can only be accomplished when the student has a complete understanding of the subject.

Organization plays an equally important part in the preparation of the essay answer. Just as a house must have a planned foundation so also must your essay answer have a planned framework. An instructor who is forced to read a jumbled mass of information is inclined to grade down such a poorly organized paper. An essay answer demands a planned outline. This outline may be either worked out in the mind or jotted down on a blank page in the examination book.

Selection of the material for your answer will come from your knowledge of the subject and your intelligence. A well-prepared student should be able to write for a great length of time on a good essay question. Since examinations have a time limit it is the student's obligation to select only the essential material for his answer. This requires a complete knowledge of the subject and a common-sense ability to distinguish between the important and the unimportant.

Factual knowledge is also important for a good answer to an essay question. The answer that contains the greatest amount of factual material that is well organized will receive the highest grade from the instructor.

The following essay questions should be answered after keeping in mind the above four points. The essay questions listed below cover chapter by chapter the material found in the text.

A. *General Essay Questions*.

1. What elements of our modern civilization were contributed by the Middle Ages? Can you think of any modern institutions which are not in some way derived from medieval institutions?
2. Discuss the development of the English parliament under Edward III. How did the war facilitate the rise of parliament? Why did parliament succeed when the Estates General failed?
3. Compare the attitude of the Hapsburgs with that of the Luxemburgs in regard to Italy and the imperial pretensions.
4. Describe the Albigensian Crusade and show the effects thereof upon both northern and southern France.
5. Contrast the size of the medieval town with that of the modern. Locate in your own vicinity towns the same size as Venice, Ghent, London, in the thirteenth century.
6. Name the chief twelfth-century universities and tell in what study each excelled.
7. Compare the success of Innocent III in his interventions in Germany, England and France.
8. Why was the siege of Antioch the chief event of the first crusade? Why was the conquest of Antioch necessary before Jerusalem could be taken?
9. What were the elements of strength and weakness in the position of the Capetian kings of France?
10. What is the significance of the Moslem conquests in the his-

tory of the church; in the history of Spain; in the history of the Byzantine Empire.

11. Discuss the governmental institutions under Charlemagne; how did his reforms facilitate the development of feudalism?

12. Compare the civilization of Bagdad with that of Byzantium and with that of the Frankish West about 800.

13. Explain the Hohenstaufen-Guelf rivalry, its causes and effects on Germany and on Italy.

14. Name the chief 12th century universities and tell in what study each excelled.

15. How does the career of John of Salisbury disprove the old theory that classical studies and the humanities were neglected in the Middle Ages?

Specific Essay Questions.

Chapter I

1. Discuss the causes which motivated Diocletian to reform the empire.

2. In what respects did the Roman paganism fail to meet the needs of the Romans in the late empire?

3. Why did the decline of the *curioles* and the establishment of the *colonate* facilitate the subsequent collapse of the empire?

Chapter II.

1. Discuss the causes for the persecution of the Christians before Diocletian.

2. What were the motives of Constantine in accepting Christianity?

3. What were the Judaic origins of Christianity?

4. List the causes for the spread of Christianity.

Chapter III.

1. Discuss the "peaceful" penetration of the empire by the Germans.

2. What was the real significance of the "fall" in 476?

3. Explain the importance of Germanic Law.

4. Compare the degree of Romanization in the various German kingdoms.

Chapter IV.

1. Identify: Alaric, Ataulf, Attila, Zeno, Orestes, Theodoric the Ostrogoth, Ulfilas, Wergeld, Clovis, Odoacer.

2. Discuss fully the barbarian invasions of Britain.

3. "The rise of Clovis gave rise to the great Merovingian Frankish kingdom." Discuss this statement.

Chapter V.

1. When and why did the late Roman Empire become the Byzantine?
2. Enumerate and describe the parts of the *Corpus Juris Civilis*.
3. Identify: Justin I, Theodora, Narses, Totila, Belisarius.

Chapter VI.

1. Trace briefly the relations of the popes with the Lombard monarchs.
2. Identify: St. Patrick, St. Columba, St. Boniface, Gregory I, Donation of Pepin.
3. Compare and contrast the Irish and the Roman missionary movements.

Chapter VII.

1. Enumerate the chief teachings of the Mohammed and compare them with those of Judaism and Christianity.
2. Discuss the importance of the civil war between Ali and Muawija.
3. To what extent can the sudden expansion of the Arabs be attributed to religious and to what extent to economic and social causes?

Chapter VIII.

1. Identify: Charles Martel, Carloman, Tassilo, Battle of Tours, Pope Stephen II.
2. Discuss the relative position of the Kings and the Mayors of the Palace at the time of Charles Martel.
3. Trace the relations between the papacy and the Frankish monarchs from Charles Martel's accession to power until the death of Charlemagne.

Chapter IX.

1. What lands were visited by the Norsemen and what permanent settlements made?
2. What caused the Norse invasions?
3. Compare the barbarian invasions of the 5th century with those of the 9th century.

Chapter X.

1. Explain the rise of the Saxon monarchy in Germany.
2. Discuss fully the acquisition of Italy by Otto I.
3. Why did the Otto's have control of the Papacy?

Chapter XI.

1. Define: Fief, homage, fealty, vassal, lord, aids, escheat, domain, tenure, relief.
2. How did the feudal lord finance himself?
3. Differentiate between the manorial and the feudal systems.

4. Discuss the economic, personal and political characteristics of the possession of a fief.

Chapter XII.

1. Identify: Lay investiture, Cluny, Rise of Patavia, Concordat of Worms, Guelfs.
2. Explain the Hohenstaufen-Guelf rivalry, its causes and effects on Germany and on Italy.
3. What might have been the effect on empire and papacy had Frederick not protested the *beneficium* in the letter of Adrian IV?

Chapter XIII.

1. What were the causes and results of the Second and Third Crusades?
2. Trace the events of the Fourth Crusade through the final conquest of Constantinople.
3. How does the Fourth Crusade, in contrast with the First, show the change in the motives of the crusaders?

Chapter XIV.

1. Discuss the theory of the origin of the town in the merchant colony.
2. How were the town charters obtained?
3. What conditions favored the growth of towns in Italy and Germany?

Chapter XV.

1. What was the temporal power of the Church in the 12th and 13th centuries?
2. Identify: St. Francis of Assisi, Cistercians, Sacraments, Canon Law, Peter Abelard.
3. List and explain three heretical movements as classified by the Catholic Church.

Chapter XVI.

1. Describe the organization and curricula of the medieval university.
2. Discuss the career of Peter Abelard.
3. Name the chief 12th century universities and tell in what study each excelled.

Chapter XVII.

1. What part did Innocent III play in the Disputed Election of 1198?
2. Discuss Frederick II's crusade.
3. Explain the Sicilian Vespers of 1282.

Chapter XVIII.

1. Describe the breakdown of the curia regis in England under Henry II.

2. Contrast Philip Augustus and Richard the Lion Hearted in character and accomplishments.

3. Name and locate the chief fiefs of France at the time of Louis VI.

Chapter XIX.

1. What were the causes of the Hundred Years' War, political, economic and dynastic?

2. Divide the Hundred Years' War into four main periods. What were the chief events and the results of each?

3. How do you explain the success of Joan d'Arc? What position did she hold in the army? What was her power?

Chapter XX.

1. Describe the effect of the Avignon papacy on the attitude of Europe toward the Church and on the papacy itself.

2. Trace anti-clericalism in England and show how the Avignon papacy permitted John Wycliffe to attack the papacy and launch upon his heresies.

3. To what extent was the Hussite movement a nationalist movement among the Czechs?

Chapter XXI.

1. Compare the attitude of the Hapsburgs with that of the Luxemburgs in regard to Italy and the imperial pretensions.

2. Compare the map of Germany in 1272 with that in 1438; what states have arisen, and what new houses?

3. What was the purpose of the Hanseatic League? How was it organized?

Chapter XXII.

1. How was the unification of Spain accomplished?

2. What was the effect on Spain of the expulsion of the Moors from Granada?

3. What were the motives of Prince Henry the Navigator, and what were the results of his efforts?

Chapter XXIII.

1. From what sources did Dante derive his ideas of Heaven, of Hell?

2. What do we mean by Humanism?

3. What elements of our modern civilization were contributed by the Middle Ages?

BIBLIOGRAPHY

Chapter I.
1. *Cambridge Medieval History*, I, 642-667.
2. Rostovtzeff, *Rome*, 351-366.
3. Munro and Sellery, *Medieval Civilization*, 18-33.

Chapter II.
1. Lot, *End of the Ancient World*, 86-99.
2. Dill, *Roman Society in the Last Century*, 3-112.
3. Bury, *Barbarian Invasions*, 3-20.

Chapter III.
1. Orman, *Dark Ages*, 55-64.
2. Villari, *Barbarian Invasions*, 150-191.
3. Thompson, *Middle Ages*, 81-121.

Chapter IV.
1. Bradley, *The Story of the Goths*.
2. Funck-Brentano, *Earliest Times*, 210-249.
3. Gregory of Tours, *History of the Franks*.

Chapter V.
1. *Cambridge Medieval History*, II, 53-108.
2. Munro and Sellery, *Medieval Civilization*, 87-114.
3. Diehl, *Byzantine Empire*, 40-52.

Chapter VI.
1. Scott, Hyma, Noyes, *Readings*, 77-92.
2. *Cambridge Medieval History*, II, 496-542.
3. Thompson, *Middle Ages*, 190-218.

Chapter VII.
1. Moss, *Birth of the Middle Ages*, 149-174.
2. Muir, *Life of Mohammed*, Chap., 3, 7, 37.
3. Gilman, *The Saracens*, 34-207.

Chapter VIII.
1. Einhard, *Life of Charlemagne*, 180-235.
2. Bryce, *Holy Roman Empire*, Chap. 5.
3. *Cambridge Medieval History*, II, 595-630.

Chapter IX.
1. Haskins, *The Normans in European History*, 26-51.
2. Thompson, *Middle Ages*, 306-330.
3. *Cambridge Medieval History*, III, 309-339.

Chapter X.
1. Emerton, *Middle Ages*, 115-172.
2. Tout, *Empire and Papacy*, 12-65.
3. *Cambridge Medieval History* III, 179-214.

Chapter XI.
1. Thompson, *Middle Ages*, 688-708.
2. Round, *Feudal England*, 225-314.
3. Seignobos, *The Feudal Regime*, 71-88.

Chapter XII.
1. Tout, *Empire and Papacy*, 221-244.
2. Scott, Hyma, Noyes, *Readings*, 249-252.
3. *Cambridge Medieval History* V, 334-359.

Chapter XIII.
1. Thompson, *Middle Ages*, 561-601.
2. Adams, *Civilization in the Middle Ages*, 254-273.
3. Munro and Sontag, *Middle Ages*, 241-255.

Chapter XIV.
1. Heaton, *Economic History*, 132-147.
2. Pirenne, *Medieval Citus*, 56-77.
3. Stephenson, *Borough on Town*, 22-46.

Chapter XV.
1. Schaff, *History of the Christian Church*, V, 764-811.
2. Lagarde, *The Latin Church in the Middle Ages*, 126-184.
3. Scott, Hyma, Noyes, *Readings*, 399-405.

Chapter XVI.
1. McCabe, *Peter Abelard*.
2. Haskins, *The Rise of the Universities*.
3. Taylor, *Medieval Mind*, II, 133-175.

Chapter XVII.
1. Villari, *Medieval Italy*, 270-286.
2. Emerton, *Middle Ages*, 314-356.
3. *Cambridge Medieval History*, VI, 80-109.

Chapter XVIII.
1. Cheynuy, *Dawn of a New Era*, 176-180.
2. Lodge, *Close of the Middle Ages*, 43-62.
3. Tout, *England, 1216-1377*, 1-288.

Chapter XIX.
1. Emerton, *Beginnings of Modern Europe*, 252-310.
2. Lunt, *History of England*, 232-260.
3. Macdonald, *History of France*, I, 219-317.

Chapter XX.
1. *Cambridge Medieval History*, VII, 486-507.
2. Workman, *John Wycliffe*.
3. Waugh, *Europe, 1378-1494*, 208-239.

Chapter XXI.
   1. *Cambridge Medieval History*, VI, 362-392.
   2. Bryce, *Holy Roman Empire*, Chap. 14.
   3. Zimmern, *The Hansa Towns*.
Chapter XXII.
   1. Waugh, *Europe, 1378-1494*, 378-401.
   2. Chapman, *History of Spain*, I, 298-390.
   3. Martins, *Iberian Civilization*, 139-181.
Chapter XXIII.
   1. Lucas, *Renaissance and Reformation*, 193-217.
   2. *Cambridge Medieval History*, VII, 751-776.
   3. Taylor, *Medieval Mind*, II, 555-590.

INDEX

A

Abbasid Dynasty, 42
Abelard, Peter, 93, 98
Acre, 80, 82
Adelard of Bath, 101
Adrianople, Castle of, 4, 21
Aëtius, Roman general, 25
Africa, 22
Africanus, Constantinus, 100
Agnes, Empress, 67
Aistulf, King, 39
Alarie, 12, 22
Alberti, 151
Albigensians, 94, 115
Albion, 28
Alexander II, Pope, 68
Alexander V, Pope, 134
Alexandria, 12
Alfonso VI, Castile, 75
Alfred, the Great, 51
Alighieri, Dante, 102
Allemani, 20, 26
Almoravide, 75
Ambrose, Saint, 14
Angler, 24
Anglo-Saxon, Chronicle, 101
Anselm, Saint, 98
Ansgar, Saint, 53
Antioch, 31
Apostles, 8
Aquileia, 23
Aquinas, Thomas, Saint, 98
Aquitaine, Duke of, 65
Arabic, Empire, 39, 41
Arc, Joan of, 125
Arcadius, Emperor, 29
Architecture, Gothic, 95
Arianism, 13, 33
Aristotle, 98
Arius, Alexandria of, 13
Arkhan, Sultan, 143
Armagnacs, 123
Artevelde, James Van, 120

Ataulf, 22
Athanasius, Saint, 13
Attila, 23, 24
Augusti, 3
Augustine, Saint, 13, 14, 22, 55, 92
Augustus, Philip, 16, 99
Austrasia, 26, 43
Avars, 30
Aversa, 68
Avignon, Papacy, 130

B

Babylonian Captivity, 130
Bacon, Roger, 101
Baillis, 115
Baldwin, Count of Flanders, 77
Balliol, Edward, 121
Baltic, Germany, 15
Barbarossa in Germany, 73; in Italy, 72
Basel, Council of, 135
Basil, Saint, 12
Bavaria, 26
Becket, St. Thomas, 112
Bede, Venerable, 35, 101
Belisarius, 27
Benedict I, Pope, 34
Benedict XI, Pope, 118
Benedict XIII, Pope, 134
Benedict, of Nursia, Saint, 34
Benedictine, Monasticism, 34
Benedictine, Rule, 34, 44
Beneficium, 60
Beowulf, 101
Bernard, of Clairvaux, Saint, 92
Berno, 65
Besancon, the Incident, 73
Black Death, 121
Black Prince, 123
Blanche, of Castille, 115
Boethius, 96
Bohemond, 77
Boniface, Saint, 37, 38, 44
Boniface, VIII, Pope, 118, 130